MW00880491

Absolute Abundance

Your Power to Realize a more abundant life now

Matthew F. Bennett A.l.c.

Matura Nath Das Adhikari

Absolute Abundance

Other books by the author:

Tales of the East

Dharma of Abundance

Journey to Fulfillment

For more information or to schedule a private consultation.

Please visit

www.abundantlives.org

Copyright © 2014 by Matthew F. Bennett

All rights reserved. No part of this book may be reproduced in any form or by any means, electronic or mechanical, including photocopying, recording, or by any information storage and retrieval system, without permission in writing from the publisher.

ISBN-13:978-1492396260

Absolute Abundance

To my beloved Gurudeva,
Srila Bhakti Rakshaka Sridhar Deva Goswami,
the emperor of Sanyasi Kings who, even at a very advanced age,
shared so much wisdom and affection. I am also grateful to
His Divine Servitor Srila Bhakti Sundar Govinda Maharaja
who was the personification of humility, wisdom and kindness.
My further gratitude to my friends and family who inspired me to teach,
write and share the nectar that was collected through
many years of service.

blessed art thou upon the swan

the essence of divine sound
and everlasting beauty

inspiration of the speaker
poet & priest

the creator's beloved
and friend of the pure

your hands bear the vina
the book and the beads

while granting a boon
fulfilling our needs

an image auspicious
bright halo enshrined

grant us thy mercy
benevolence divine

CONTENTS

INTRODUCTION

Thank you for taking the time to read this book. It's a subject that fascinates me and I'm sure will inspire you as well. Every investment in ourselves brings a return of growth and new ability. Congratulations to you for taking the time to invest in your understanding of yourself! I think it's the best investment you can make because I'm convinced that success and abundance begin with self-understanding.

One of the great truths that have come to light in the modern age is that we can no longer escape the knowledge that our interior lives and our exterior circumstances reflect each other. As a person thinks, so they are, or soon will be.

The basic premise of this book is that abundance is a state of mind. Not just material abundance, but spiritual abundance. Enthusiasm is a form of this abundance, and it fuels every other energetic pattern in our lives.

Everyone is seeking fulfillment, happiness and satisfaction in life. Most of us have heard of the Law of Attraction, or the concept of like attracts like. Although such concepts are again popular, these types of ideas have been around a long time. They are rooted in the deepest understanding of the human mind. This book explains these concepts and so much more. It's the fruit of my life-long search for meaning. It's not just a book filled with information, it's a book filled with practical wisdom, which, when applied, can transform your life. No one is a perfected being. We are are all works in progress. I've been graced with some understanding for the time being and now I'd like to share it with you.

Abundance is not my ability to acquire and guard anything *from* change, but rather, my realization that true abundance is linked to my inner harmony *with* change, and that I am surrounded by immense amounts of flowing energy and information. This realization is true abundance. This flow represents living opportunity, and opportunity is the gateway to inner abundance as well as financial wealth.

Increase the flow and the flow will increase.

The constant change inherent in the world's vast field of energy and information does not represent loss, but transformation, and transformation is flow; it is currency; it is life and that means opportunity, fresh experience and new rewards.

The environment is conscious and responsive to the movements of my own localized consciousness and by harmoniously participating in the flow of this vast movement of energy and information I enter into a relationship of true abundance and satisfaction.

To understand that one's outer circumstances are vitally linked to one's inner representations is a wish-fulfilling gem of wisdom, a rare philosopher's stone of immense value. Our search for such a deep realization is the Magnum Opus of the human race.

Positive inner representations, selfless service and compassion are powerful tools for our inner growth. Paradoxically, by giving more of myself, I attain more inner satisfaction. Giving increases the flow from me, which also opens the channel for flow towards me. If I'm unwilling to share and give, if I'm too attached and unwilling to let go of people and things, I'm choking the energetic flow towards myself as well.

Life will always test our sincerity, and there will always be challenges, but the answer is not for us to build a seemingly protective fortress of money, strength, fame or emotional distance. For all-powerful time will wash all of these away.

The answer lies within our own unassailable consciousness, the deepest ground of our being, which is the seat of pure awareness, satisfaction and wisdom.

Faith is the doorway to this understanding and realization.

The progress of this transformation begins with our own mindfulness and self-awareness coupled with the elegant governance of our own inner states of consciousness. Whatever is happening to us at this moment is integrally linked to how we perceive and represent reality to ourselves.

As the philosopher Bishop Berkeley famously stated, *"The world is in the mind."* You began this exciting adventure long ago.

Read your life with a relaxed curiosity and an open heart. Remain open to the infinite possibilities of life. A dogmatic obsession with only one kind of meaning forecloses the creative potential of any given experience.

Allow wisdom to effortlessly arise in the simple radiance of your being. Listen to your heart. Practice daily until it becomes a living expression of your own abundant life. Then pass it on...

CHAPTER ONE
THE POWER OF CLARITY

"More important than the quest for certainty
is the quest for clarity."
- Francois Gautieror

ABUNDANCE DEFINED

Just what is abundance? The dictionary defines it as a great plentiful amount. Abundance is fullness, to overflowing, affluence and wealth. Personally, I choose to define abundance as potentiality. Potentiality is the inherent wealth in objective or circumstantial possibility. Abundance is its probability and productivity in motion.

More importantly, abundance is flow, the free movement of energy and information. We are surrounded by this abundance in the forms of financial abundance, emotional abundance, energetic abundance and resourceful abundance, which constantly flows from the conscious source, the zero point, the quantum field, or what theologians and the faithful call divinity — the ultimate and unlimited source of all spiritual and material abundance. It is the Universal Mind and the all-pervading consciousness that is the matrix of all material manifestation. Within all beings is conscious source as *jiv-atma*, or conscious, non-material self. When this *jiv-atma* realizes its abundance in relation to the *param-atma*, the sum total of consciousness, it approaches its full potentiality in absolute abundance. The connecting link is faith, love, and dedication, its fruit is the realization of unity in diversity. Abundance is possibility, and your success flows from the recognition of this possibility backed by your consistent action. In other words, your dynamic harmony with living, moving, conscious potentiality is a dynamic state of success, and I define success as the unbounded ability to take dynamic action. Abundance is also the ability to recognize the abundant potentialities that surround us at every moment.

Everyone wants to experience happiness and an abundant state of inner-freedom of uninhibited exaltation. Yet we often mistake material accumulation and achievement as the means, when in actuality it is simplicity and release that affect the true emergence of joy. If we put clarity first, then great potentiality and abundant thinking are sure to follow. Clarity is power and the power that comes from clarity is unstoppable.

From this clarity of perception our receptivity to a greater potential gradually awakens and we begin to not merely wish but actually realize that a greater abundance in all areas of our lives is possible. This sets up the structural foundation for a paradigm of present moment abundance, which is the budding stage of manifestation.

When you are feeling vibrant, awake and joyfully alive, you will begin to realize you are surrounded by opportunity, change and abundance. Your communication to yourself and others will improve and your success will be measured by an increased willingness to take consistent action in cultivating these opportunities.

As I said earlier, the dictionary defines abundance as a great or plentiful amount...of something. Just what is the most abundant thing we have great and plentiful amounts of?

The answer of course is experience. No matter who you are, what you are doing or what your life has been, you have an incredible amount of experience. Every thought, word and deed of your life has been recorded within your subconscious mind. Hypnosis has revealed that copious amounts of detailed perception can be drawn up from the subconscious about any particular event. The totality of your sensory experience is lying fallow below your conscious mind. It's a vast amount of information that only the spaciousness of consciousness could contain. Now, what you actually do with all that experience is another matter. Does it transform you? Yes, absolutely! But how? Is it an empowering transformation? Does it excite you about life and compel you towards more meaningful action or do you feel victimized by experiences? I'm convinced that your personal experiences have more to do with your own perceptions and inner representations than the environment. We'll be going over this concept many times because it is a fundamental key to your liberation into a more abundant spiritual and material experience of life.

We all have perceptual filters through which we intellectually and emotionally filter and weigh each experience we encounter. Some of these filters are operating unconsciously in the background, unnoticed by our conscious mind but registered by emotion, feelings, or unconscious actions.

SPIRITUAL PSYCHOLOGY AND THE SELF

The three primary perceptual filters operating in most people are intimately linked to how we view ourselves; in other words, our self-image, self-esteem and the resulting self-confidence of image and esteem. This self-image is a largely unconscious mental representation we have of ourselves that is basically a fabrication of the conditioned mind. Spiritual traditions of the East call this the false-ego. It is a mental projection that colors our consciousness and is constituted largely of ideas and experiences that were internalized in our formative years and reinforced through our identification with them. It is also a type of perceptual filter, operating unconsciously.

This false internal representation of self, when confused with the true conscious individual, will necessarily limit our productivity and sense of what's possible because it dramatically falls short of who we are in reality.

For example, imagine if you had a full-size cardboard representation of yourself, like the ones you see of actors displayed in the video stores. Just suppose you carried that facsimile around in front of you everywhere you went. Imagine that no one related with you, the actual person behind the cardboard man or woman, but only took you at face value. Seems absurd, but this is similar to what's going on energetically when we consider the vast difference in potentiality between the actual inner conscious individual and the misrepresentation of false-ego that is linked to the limitations of past experiences, other peoples opinions and our identifications with this physical body of limited manifestation.

The fundamental basis of absolute abundance begins from the foundation of spiritual self-knowledge. Your inner, deeper identity in spiritual consciousness is the sentient projector of conscious awareness that is hidden in the background of your being, yet provides the illuminating quality that energizes the outer layers or systems of "self" such as the mind, intellect, senses and body.

Consider the two following paragraphs and their implications as to what is possible and probable for you.

"I am a biological organism composed of physical elements.
My mind and emotions are merely the play of chemicals.
I will live for less than 100 years and then vanish."

or

"I am a pure point of conscious light,
a conscious awareness without beginning or end.
I am unlimited in my conscious potentiality."

Can you see the vast difference in potentiality and quality of the two statements? Examine the energetic and psychological basis from which you consciously or unconsciously operate your life. It makes a huge difference to you on all levels in terms of quality and experience.

Again, clarity is the power, and the power of clarity is unstoppable.

This conception of the non-material conscious self is neither fantasy nor religious dogma. This is deep cognitive science, and the basis of unfettered spirituality, supported by thousands of years of culture, tradition and experience. We can't empirically measure consciousness but everyone is experiencing its reality everyday. It's the subtle-most energy, more subtle than mind or intellect. The subtlest energies are often the most potent, like the atom. We can't measure or physically verify the emotional states of love, hate, faith or hope, yet we subjectively know they exist and exert great impact upon our lives. So the immeasurably subtle is not necessarily un-scientific, or unverifiable. It is just so delicate as to be difficult to analyze or measure.

Mind is the penumbra of the conscious self and intellect is the discerning function of the mind. Try to acquaint yourself with these ideas. Explore the vast amount of traditional and modern knowledge in this regard and go within yourself and separate and detach your inner self through observation and meditation. Through meditation and insight detach your conscious awareness from the mind, intellect, thoughts and emotions. The great power of your conscious self lies hidden behind these mental representations. It is confusion of self with mind and emotion that disempowers your life from its absolute abundance. It is the magnificent power of inner clarity that restores that abundant potentiality. Clarity clears away that which clouds our inner perception.

In reality, you are indeed a pure point of conscious light, a conscious awareness without beginning or end. You are unlimited in your conscious potentiality.

As I stated in the introduction, abundance is a state of mind. It's all about how you perceive and represent experience to yourself. In fact, all of our life experiences begin within our own conscious awareness, for in reality, life is subjective. What makes an experience good or bad has more to do with our perception and interpretation of the experience than the actual event. What's coming at you is largely coming from within you. What I'd like to further share with you is the fact that perception and experience are the most abundant resources we have available. But the important factor is what we do with these resources and how we actually manage them in our daily life. This determines whether we are actually living our life from a fulfilling and abundant perspective.

UNDERSTANDING THE MIND

The conscious mind is our waking state that we experience throughout our day. In this area of the mind we think, we reason, and generally process the information that we receive through our five knowledge-acquiring senses, such as the eyes, ears, nose, mouth and skin. The mind in general is the subtle penumbra surrounding the spiritual core of our being, which is our non-material self, the nature of which is unassailable existence, sentience and bliss.

The presence of consciousness in the mind and body is indicated by three symptoms, which are thinking, feeling and willing. These are generally experienced through the conscious mind.

The senses are like windows allowing perceptual energy to flow into the area of the conscious mind, as well as mental energy to flow out in projection upon the objects of the senses. Once sense impressions are received in the mind, these perceptual impressions are deliberated upon by the intelligence and reason, which are the critical factors of our higher cognitive awareness. Mental energy can also leak out through the senses when we are inattentive where we place our attention, or when we obsess over an object or person, or attach our own projected representations upon objects, people and circumstances.

There is much perceptual information that enters our mind without our conscious awareness and these unseen perceptions can unconsciously effect our apparently conscious decisions without our understanding. Subliminal advertising and hypnosis often employ this type of perceptual bypass methodology.

Now whatever you think, feel, do and say creates a psychic impression in the mind. The sum total of all your perceptual experiences in life have been recorded in your unconscious mind. Many of these attitudes and states are silently housed in our unconscious mind and have formed complexes of idea-links that connect thoughts and feelings to other similar states. These psychic links lay dormant but are often emotionally charged. They are often activated by triggers that are linked stimulants that awaken them. These triggers act like buttons that activate and release the energy of these hidden emotional states. A simple way to understand their operation is in connection with music. As a young child I heard many Beatle songs. Those songs always made me feel happy, and it was a happy time of life, and as a result, I unconsciously linked emotionally pleasant states in my unconscious mind with the song as the trigger. Now, forty years later I can hear one of those songs and it will without fail awaken a pleasant emotional state within me. The song is a trigger to the state. We do this all the time with many types of experiences becoming linked to varying states of happiness and distress and everything in between. Negative emotional triggers are sometimes the strongest because of the intensity of the emotions linked to them. We have to be on the lookout for these if we wish to take control of our own inner states and become happier and more emotionally balanced individuals.

We unconsciously wire our emotions and psychology by linking stimulus and state. Fortunately we can become aware of this situation and take conscious control of these processes to empower ourselves to more elegant forms of expression. Through clarity of consciousness we can begin to observe the various stimulus and responses that make up our daily experiences.

Many marriages get into trouble because the partners may have disagreements about the various emotionally charged topics that couples deal with, such as sex, money and work. In the midst of these disagreements they are often looking directly into the face of their partner and listening intently to their voice. This can unintentionally create a negative emotional trigger of the face and voice of the partner.

Over time there can be a residual build-up of these triggers to the point where all you have to do is look at your partner's face or hear his voice and a negative emotional response arises. Like for example, when she leaves the cap off the toothpaste and you become irrationally irate. You negatively over-react due to the build up of repressed negative emotions. In reality, it is actually your responsibility to control your emotional state, not her responsibility to behave in ways that don't irritate you. Often couples that have been together for decades have these types of experiences. Usually, one of three modalities will become prominent, such as the auditory trigger. Others who are more visually oriented will be more effectively stimulated by what they see, and many have their triggers centered in feeling, or any combination of all three.

Work with these ideas. They will grow stronger with practice. By practicing non-judgmental observation you will experience greater clarity and become more skilled in taking control of your mental states. In time you will develop a greater command of yourself and your responses to the events in your life. You'll be delighted by the difference it makes in the quality of your relationships and experiences. You'll feel a new and profound calm as you realize that you can pick and choose how and when you respond to others. And you can respond playfully for their benefit rather than bitterly to your own detriment.

Occasionally you will encounter someone who blows up on you because you are not responding to his or her cues. This is an interesting experience, and don't be alarmed. It doesn't mean you're being insensitive. When done skillfully, even playfully, with an underlying understanding and affection, it can be a magnificent lesson in human nature, for the both of you. Here's an example from my own experience.

EMOTIONAL IMPASSE

I was once involved in a property management dispute that escalated into a turf war. My neighbor began harassing me night and day. At the outset I was very disturbed because no matter how patient and calm I tried to remain his aggression loomed large in my daily experience. Finally I detached myself emotionally from the situation with the realization that he could do nothing to harm or bother me if I didn't emotionally allow it. This was a turning point. To my amazement, it seemed that the calmer and more patient I became, the more angry and irritable he became (you see, I was no longer intimidated by his anger, nor would I respond to his anger cues in the compliant way he desired me to). Finally I sat him down and told him that his emotional instability was his concern, not mine.

When he heard this, he literally blew his top and had an emotional meltdown, sobbing right in front of me. Seeing his vulnerability awakened my compassion and I was totally free of him at that point. He eventually realized he had no emotional leverage on me and moved out. I felt compassion for him and his associates because they could never deal with their own emotional states. They were bitterly dedicated to changing and defeating me, blaming my very presence for their unhappiness. What an unhealthy way to live. You see as long as you dislike someone, you are mentally and emotionally linked to them. Carrying negative emotions is like carrying poison in your life. They fester from within and eat away at you from the inside, eventually producing the physical symptoms of disease, decay and mental fatigue.

Fortunately for me, the grudge and accompanying negative emotional block resided in them, not me. Through forgiveness I am free of them. Emotional negativity is a state of decay and it's only a matter of time before it shows up in the physical organism.

So you see, when two people meet, the one with greater psychological maturity and poise will always be in a better and healthier position. It's not a power trip. It's a practical understanding that will assist you to become a happier and calmer person regardless of your circumstances and the people around you.

In order to override past conditioning and refresh ourselves with new and more beneficial states, and the more elegant actions that follow, we need to give better quality perceptions to our minds. Think of it as sowing a garden. Whatever seed-thoughts you place in your mind, those seeds will grow to produce a sweet or bitter fruit. It's your choice. Why not work for your own well being?

MANAGING INNER STATES

We all suffer tragedy and loss. We all experience difficulty in relationships from time to time. None are immune to suffering. It's the human condition. But we ourselves decide what it means to us. Any experience, regardless of its nature, can be viewed as an opportunity to grow and learn. Difficulties are part of the landscape here in the material world. Difficulties are lessons for growth, not punishments for sins. They remind us that the deeper purpose of life is to grow our inner insight and love. When there is pain in your body it is an indication that the physical organism is out of balance somewhere. Similarly, when there is pain or difficulty in your life, it is a message that you are out of harmony with yourself. Inner adjustment is necessary and a proactive daily approach involving your personal inner growth will remove many of the potentially difficult causes before they appear in your life as effects, and its always easier to deal with causes than it is to clean up the effects.

By taking control of your inner states, you reclaim the power to experience life on your own terms, not someone else's. We can't change the past, but we can alter its impact upon us in the present. We do this most effectively by changing the way we represent it to ourselves. This applies to past, present and future as well. Manage your mental states in the present and you've effectively mastered the past and future. Control in the present is where the true power lies. Here's a short mantra I composed:

"Think about the way you think, for thinking makes it so. For every thought you think about another seed you sow."

Psychological content can be altered by modifying the modalities of its internal representation.

REFRAMING THOUGHTS

Yes, the emotional impact of any inner representation can be diminished or increased in a positive or negative way by altering its modalities. Is it big and bright? Move it into the distance and put a grey tone on it. Is it loud and in your face? Minimize it and turn down the volume. Alter its shape and size. Is it scary? Make it funny, warm and fuzzy, small and cuddly. Attach a new and more positive emotional charge to it and you will feel differently about it. We can decide how we represent ideas within our own mental system, and we can decide what defines the value of our lives and in turn, what we become. That power is our own internal choice, not the whim of circumstance. The science of Neurolinguistic Programming and Jungian psychology both deal extensively with these subject matters. Research these ideas and apply them in all areas of your experience. As I said before, it's always easier to deal with causes than it is to clean up the effects. Whatever you are going through at present could have been avoided by greater insight at the outset.

The good news is that we can take control of these mental processes and use them to our benefit by programming positive, constructive and insightful states with visual and auditory triggers as the cues of our choice.

OPPORTUNITY MEETS PREPARATION

In my twenties, I was working as an art director at a prominent research publishing company in Menlo Park, California. You could say that I was nearing a high point in my life that had been preceded by a remarkable series of events.

Just a few years earlier I had been earning a minimum wage, working in a commercial film lab with dangerous chemicals and not so favorable association. This was way before digital and we were using harsh chemicals to process microfilm records for banks and various corporate accounts. We also had a silver recovery system that chemically separated the trace amounts of silver from the film emulsion and electrostatically gathered a thick layer of silver to a spinning drum. It was an interesting process but as an entry-level environment without strict supervision it was steeped in drug use, loud music and unhealthy toxic conditions.

One day, feeling dissatisfaction with my employment in the lab, I began casually perusing the want ads in the San Francisco Chronicle. Running down the columns, an ad that eventually caught my eye was to lead me into experiences that would dramatically change my life. It was an opening for a junior illustrator position in a market research publishing firm called Gnostic Concepts Inc., located in an affluent outlying area of Silicon Valley called Menlo Park. Not only did it pay substantially more than what I was currently making, it was an upscale professional office environment peopled by progressive, educated and successful people. Classical music was the predominant vibration, and to top it off my beautiful girlfriend Jill lived just a few blocks away! Abundant opportunity number one!

I called that ad straight away and arranged for an interview. I was excited and motivated but unsure if I was totally prepared for the position because I had no experience in business matters or in technical illustration. But I did have enthusiasm, and powered by twenty-something spunk and sheer optimism, I showed up for the interview. Another great asset that I brought along was my portfolio of drawings and paintings. I had been drawing since an early age and had a reluctance to throw anything away, so by this time I had amassed a large collection of original art.

In high school and college I was drawn to the works of the old masters and was particularly attracted to the work of Albrecht Durer, a fifteenth century master etcher and wood carver. His detailed line drawings had been inspiring my own art for years. The work in my portfolio reflected his style of intricate ink renderings. Well, this was a great and abundant synchronicity because when the art director saw my portfolio she immediately appreciated my artistic ability (as she was a fine artist as well) and realized that based on my pen and ink work, I had the necessary ability and potential to step into the illustrator position immediately. By the end of the meeting, to my great surprise and delight she asked me when I could start!

I was astounded and overjoyed as I drove away knowing that this was one of the major turning points in my life and that I had just been economically and professionally upgraded beyond what I had ever dreamed. I said goodbye to my friends at the film lab and began wearing suits and ties, working in a beautiful office with my own drafting table and making twice the money I had before. It became clear to me that adequate preparation is a fundamental supporting factor for success, and that my love of art and years of drawing prepared me with the necessary skills to step into a greatly expanded field of possibilities, personal growth and economic increase. I had made an investment in my future by pursuing what I loved. In this case, art.

When abundant opportunity meets abundant preparation there is abundant growth, but first you have to be alert to the opportunity in order to recognize it. That means a certain amount of clarity to recognize value, and secondly, you have to act upon it and be ready to follow through with a clear plan. If I had carried the same "film lab" mentality into my new upscale work environment I would have quickly realized that I was out of my league. But because I was ripe for growth and had the necessary skills, humility and willingness to change, it was a smooth transition to a higher level, but not without a price. I had more responsibility and had to work harder but the rewards were greater as well. These were my first abundant epiphanies in the business world.

I clearly understood that my current position in the film lab was below what I was capable of personally and professionally and that led me to a dissatisfaction and restlessness that inspired me to look for new and better opportunities. At that point in my life it wasn't a clear process in my mind but the experience itself demonstrated the process. I was growing professionally and spiritually, and my eventual journey to India taught me the benefits of perceptual clarity. The fruit of this clarity is the ability to recognize value, great and abundant value, value that we often take for granted here in America and Europe.

MY PASSAGE TO INDIA

Let me tell you about my first trip to India and how it significantly changed my perception of wealth and abundance. In 1985, after four years as an illustrator, I eventually rose to the position of art director, which came with my own office and greater creative freedom. It was at this time that I planned to visit India and meet the saintly monk who would eventually become my spiritual teacher. His name was Srila Sridhar Maharaja. Over the course of the past several years I had been increasingly interested in yoga and Indian spirituality and I had been studying Srila Sridhar Maharaja's books and teachings about *Bhakti-yoga* and participating in a San Jose ashram community dedicated to publishing his lectures. Srila Sridhar Maharaja was now in his 90's, and it was my hope to meet him while there was still an opportunity to do so. He was a great Bengali saint. A 60-year monk and Sanskrit scholar. My commitment to my own spiritual realization had peaked in that year and to meet a great saint of the Vaishnava tradition of West Bengal, India would prove to be the high point of this inner quest.

I had a two-week vacation due to me at the time, so with the help of my girlfriend Jill, I pulled together the money for the flight and booked my journey for late March. Like many Americans, I had grown up with the common stereotypical image of India as poverty stricken, dirty and materially backwards. However, the past few years of studying the spiritual and cultural traditions of this vast nation had changed my perception from materially impoverished to culturally rich. So I was ready to overlook the surface appearances and seek the deeper wealth still living in the rich traditional culture and especially, the hearts of the beautiful Indian people. I had realized a dramatic paradigm shift and through the clarity that came through contact with Indian culture I began to recognize the immense value inherent in the ancient wisdom traditions of India.

I traveled alone, taking a late night flight from San Francisco to Singapore and then on to the city of Kolkata situated on the east coast of India. The Kolkata airport in those days was an austere affair and as soon as I stepped off the plane, and experienced my first blast of intense tropical heat, I knew I was in for something dramatically new. When I stepped outside the airport for the first time I had one of the biggest culture shocks of my life as I rode in the taxi through the streets of Kolkata on my way to Howrah Train Station. Along the way, I was amazed by the sights, smells and experiences that are the rich palette of an urban Indian city. This was my very first trip outside the United States. I was 27 and ready for abundant adventure! Crossing the Ganges River for the first time was a moment of great excitement for me and as I looked up the river's vast expanse I could feel the flow of greater possibilities and opportunities coming into in my life.

I've been to India fifteen times now and I'm still amazed at the great diversity of people and situations. I truly believe it's a photographer's paradise and riding in a cab you get to see it all. Women and children begging at the cab window, children bathing joyfully at a broken water main on a crowded corner, cows milling about everywhere and piles of trash, broken down cars and everything imaginable littering the streets. Often I would see people sleeping in the most unimaginable, noisy and crowded places. The startling juxtaposition of ancient temples adjacent to modern office buildings, holy men wandering about with stern looks on their faces and strange markings on their foreheads. Eager businessmen and annoyingly persistent, yet bright-faced children trying to sell you everything under the sun. But what really shocked me was to see the shanty-towns of black plastic roofing, makeshift filthy huts and lean-to's along walls and alleyways peopled by crippled or blind beggars and lepers with curious stringed instruments or mothers with dirty children living in the most squalid conditions. Yes, you see it all in Kolkata. Life and death in all its beautiful and horrific manifestations, in living color, and up close. Seeing all of these diverse conditions for the first time really touched my heart and helped me to see people in a new light. I could understand that all of these individuals were spiritual beings like myself evolving through a multiplicity of material and economic conditions and that their position at any given moment did not actually define who they were, but where they had been, and what they were growing out of, or into, at that particular moment in time. Compassion arose for my fellow man, woman, and child.

This experience also brought to light my own lack of appreciation for the immensely abundant life I was living in the West, and just how much I took for granted. Many who live on the streets of Kolkata only make the equivalent of $100.00 U.S. dollars per year. Whereas I regularly made that much in a day, and sometimes when conditions and opportunities are favorable I made as much as ten times that amount in a single day. India taught me a vivid lesson about value and appreciation. When I returned to the West I had new eyes that recognized the incredible abundance and opportunity that surrounded me in my everyday life.

Sometime after that initial trip, I remember one day walking down the street in my neighborhood mentally totaling up the value of the cars and homes I passed. Ten thousand...thirty thousand...two hundred thousand...five hundred thousand...It's remarkable that you can walk down any street in any American city and literally pass millions of dollars in abundant value in the form of homes and automobiles alone. Even more remarkable is how miserable and unhappy Americans can make themselves by internally misrepresenting the facts of their existence. No, happiness does not come from material wealth and possessions, but isn't it interesting that many of the most unhappy people in the world are the ones with the most money, opportunities and material abundance? By contrast, some of the most joyful and fulfilled people I've met, especially in India and Thailand, were simple villagers living in thatched roofed huts with mud floors, a cow and little else. You see, I've learned that it's not what you have, but how you have it, and often a rich cultural heritage can foster a deeper and more profoundly, yet simple happiness, a happiness far greater than the fleeting pleasures of material acquisitions of a throw-away consumer society like our own. To take this realization a step further we could say that it's not what you have, but whether you can appreciate it. And are you grateful for it?

Abundant happiness is an inside job.

Despite the challenging outward conditions many Indian people face, many that I met were totally joyful and often wise in their simplicity, a fact which I attributed to their deep spiritual culture spanning thousands of years. Granted, few are highly evolved internally to such a degree that they understand that material experience is all a passing play of energy and information, yet many if not all are acquainted with the law of karma and some flavor of spirituality that affords a deeper peek into the workings of nature and humankind. This is an almost intuitive understanding woven deeply into their ancient culture. Some are in the world, yet not of it. Many work, live and play knowing that there is a far deeper spiritual dimension to life, and that one day does not define a life, nor does one life completely define one's nature and experience in the larger picture of eternal time.

I met so many truly good, kind and generous people in India who touched my heart deeply. Like the old woman on the floor of Howrah Station clasping my ankle begging for rupees, or the exuberant children I treated to ice cream on the street, or the generous couple that welcomed a Western stranger into their very humble home and gave such a generous and heartfelt reception of hospitality that it made me want to weep for my own lack of sincere and kind generosity.

PERCEPTURAL FILTERING

This initial trip to India radically changed my view of what was possible and what was truly valuable. It was a turning point that helped me to realize that the power of perceptual filtering resides within my own consciousness and that how I represent my perceptions to myself is key in taking control of my life, as well as increasing my level of abundance and overall contentment. Perceptual filtering is a master key to realizing a far greater potential of abundant living for yourself and everyone around you. Perceptual filtering is how I represent experience to myself, in my own mind, and the values I apply to experiences.

What I learned in India gave me the practical experience that led to the understanding that when you realize that only you have the power to adjust your inner control knob of perceptual representations, you take back the power and magic of your life. A freedom and power that you may have unconsciously given away to other people, or to circumstances.

We've all played "the victim" from time to time. Blaming others for our unhappiness or lack, when the truth is that the power to be happy or abundant or fulfilled has always been ours. It resides within our own inherent nature, although perhaps hidden from our view due to emotional pain and the misconception that we must aimlessly follow our moods and attitudes wherever they lead us. Yet we do have a choice about which path to walk, be it joy or sorrow. Our beliefs about our selves and what is possible for us to achieve is another form of perceptual filtering, which determines what is possible for us in any given circumstance. Flexibility and expanding belief in what is possible, is a dynamic state of consciousness that enables us to act from our most resourceful position. Clarity of belief, choice and action support us in living more abundantly on all levels.

GENETIC PREDISPOSITIONS

In her book *Choose to be Happy,* Rima Rudner, points out that there have been several studies such as that of Dr. Richard Davidson, Ph.D., a psychologist at the University of Wisconsin, that have shown that everyone burns glucose differently in the brain. Each individual has a unique capacity to process energy, information and experience. Genetically and biologically we all have certain predispositions towards thought and behavior. Related studies have also shown that genetics play a role in determining set points of emotional stability, attitude and other psychological dispositions. This is great news because if we can clearly define the emotional and behavioral patterns and pre-dispositions of our familial and cultural backgrounds we have gained a greater insight into what we have to work with in terms of changing attitude, belief and subsequent behavior. Studies conducted on biological-identical twins by Dr. Thomas Bouchard, Ph.D., at the University of Minnesota have also revealed that twins separated at birth grow up with great psychological similarities despite diversity of environmental factors. So genetics is one piece of the puzzle. Its not everything but it does have an underlying consistency that we return to again and again.

Besides your genetic predispositions you also have various states, attitudes and biased views that you have acquired through your association with your parents, siblings, peers, mentors, teachers, idols and other significant figures in your developing life. Association is like a mirror and will reflect whatever is placed before it. Your personal psychology is a great montage of attitudes and behavioral responses that have their origins in various subconscious states. For many people, these states have been installed unknowingly in your unconsciousness through the osmosis of association with others.

Most of our attitudes about money and our ability to get it, as well as abundance in general, have been shaped by our parents and the environments and people that we were surrounded by in our early years. My own parents grew up in the time of the Great Depression and World War II and as a result they retained some residual attitudes that "life is hard" and we must "fight for what we want." Baby boomers who grew up in the expansive 50's and 60's gained a greater perspective of what was possible by the relatively more abundant attitudes that marked that post-war period of growth and prosperity, especially in America.

YOUR NATURAL LEVEL

Our predetermined genetic disposition gives us a "set point" of contentment and a corresponding attitude of "what is possible." We continually deviate from this emotional set point when we become happier than "usual" or more emotionally challenged and unhappy. But within a few days a "normal" person will generally return to their emotional set point of genetic predisposition. Persons suffering from depression may remain "off-mark" for weeks, months, or years, and this is often a symptom of another imbalance in the biology or psychology of the individual.

Our environment and associations are another important factor in determining whether we can rise above our emotional set point. But the greater factor in determining our possibility, expectancy and experience of more fulfilling states of happiness and abundance is our own cognitive ability to choose, direct and manifest greater awareness of these internal psychological states.

In the early part of the twentieth century the great electrical genius Tesla was once challenged, "Mr. Tesla, what is the value of your electricity?" To which Tesla replied; "Madam, what is the utility of a new-born baby?"

Possibility, probability, and potentiality. These three P's can become a guiding light for us. Life is a subjective experience. We impart value to the people and things around us. But beyond our relative measurements exists the unfathomable and remarkable possibilities inherent in each experience. Again, experience is abundance and how we choose to respond to our experiences and how we represent them to ourselves in our own thinking processes, as well as how we consciously choose to respond to them, determines to a greater degree our reach, abilities and capacity for happiness. More elegant responses bring about more rewarding and fulfilling relationships. We are often willing to risk more of ourselves if we believe our goal is attainable.

Right now, you have a great abundance of experiences every week, every day, every moment. How you choose to manage your response to those experiences puts the power and magic back into your life. Abundance consciousness is also the recognition of energetic flow. That flow may be represented as money, people, commodities, resources or even spiritual reality. All of these represent a flow of possibility, and possibility coupled with consistent action always brings a result. If the result is unsatisfactory then the recipe needs to be modified and acted upon until the correct result is realized in manifest form.

Abundance consciousness is also your growing ability to see value and possibility in every person, place or circumstance and intentionally choose to serve a greater good for yourself and others. We do this most effectively by diving deep into each experience and mining the inherent value concealed there as well as polishing it with sincere gratitude for the opportunity to do so.

I like to think that it's my duty to benefit others. This is somewhat akin to the Bodhisattva vow of Mahayana Buddhists. Whomever I encounter in life, I feel it is my duty to benefit them in some way. To serve everyone you meet is a wonderful practice that brings practical benefits as well. If we are merely passing by another we can mentally bless them up by sending good thoughts of health, healing and prosperity, or wishing for their spiritual growth. They may be homeless and requesting money, which I could give. Yet, to give wisely and benefit them more skillfully, I could buy them a few grocery items to hand them as I leave the parking lot. I'm not fond of giving money to people who beg on the streets because they often squander it upon cigarettes and alcohol, though I do give donations without judgment occasionally. If I give to someone who missuses the energy of money then I may just be deepening their position in ignorance. If I feed them meat, I increase their negative karma as well. Giving must be done wisely and skillfully, and then both the giver and receiver are benefitted, though the practice of giving should always be practiced. As my teacher once said: *"Practice your hand to give, even if you give a handful of ashes. Cultivate the practice of giving."*

As you grow in this broader, more liberal understanding you will begin to realize that competition is a myth and that our own ability to create value is never compromised by the presence of others. Our ability and opportunity is compromised only by our own limited beliefs, negative emotional responses and subsequent inelegant actions. Abundant living is abundant thinking, and ultimately it's the expansion of our consciousness. It's a path of emotional literacy, as well as psychological and inner spiritual growth. Optimism attracts opportunity, and opportunities make one optimistic. Everything moves in a circle.

VIBRATIONAL CONSISTENCY

Often we are puzzled, bewildered or challenged by the seemingly random succession of good and bad experiences in life. When we are dissatisfied with the results of our lives some will blame the economy, or government or society or even human nature. Yet, this misses the mark completely. It is an undeniable fact that every result has a cause, but if we are to find the deepest source of our experiences we will have to dive deep into our own consciousness.

The understanding that every experience that is coming *towards* you, is on some level coming *from* you is a phenomena that has been recently popularized as the Law of Attraction and can be further understood as the universal law of vibrational consistency. It's been here from the beginning of time and is ubiquitous and widely applicable.

Like attracts like. Everything manifest in the universe is composed of varying densities of energy and information moving in rhythmic cycles. The patterns of nature, the flow of water, clouds, seasons and even the geological landscape is moving rhythmically. The cosmos itself has a pulse and cyclic rhythm, just as the seasons move in succession. So do the planets and galaxies rotate, vibrate and rhythmically move through manifestation, growth, maintenance, decay, destruction and eventual recurring manifestation. Everything moves in a circle.

The understanding of cyclical vibrational patterns and the underlying laws of vibrational consistency helps to align us to the bigger energetic picture and from this greater vantage point we are empowered to more elegantly apply the resources of our thoughts, emotions, intelligence and actions. The old saying *"birds of a feather flock together,"* demonstrates this law of vibrational consistency. Energies that are similar will naturally be drawn together like the flock of birds, the school of fish, and the group of like-minded people.

History has shown that many similar ideas and inventions are developed simultaneously yet independently of each other in the world. Ideas are a vibrational currency that spread through humanity, sometimes spontaneously and unconsciously.

Thought is a powerful energy that is often wielded with a great deal of unconsciousness. Thoughts are the most subtle and yet most powerful vibrational energy that attracts circumstances and people into our lives. Very often it is our thoughts that attract to us the types of experiences we have on a daily basis. In this way thoughts are like magnets. Vibrational consistency works together with the law of cause and effect to bring about results in our lives.

If we are dissatisfied with the results we are currently experiencing, we need only to look to the causes in our own thinking processes. Outcomes or results have their causes in thought. My teacher once said, *"Idea is the primitive form of attainment."* Ideas attract outcomes and set energies in motion. Paradoxically, giving is the way to attract more abundance into your life because it makes room for the fresh flow of energy. Coming and going, loss and gain, increase and decrease are all varying perspectives of the same energetic flow. How we think about all this attracts what we experience.

Most parents wish their sons and daughters success. Often that success is measured by educational completion, consistency in employment, monetary abundance, long-term marital relations, healthy children, long life and a pleasant retirement. As we all know, the road towards the acquisition of each of these items is beset by multitudes of opposing forces, challenges and difficulties. It is helpful to recognize that none of these items guarantees any measure of long-range emotional or mental satisfaction. To pin one's happiness on transitory phenomena is a recipe for disappointment, because the only truly consistent phenomena in the universe is constant change. Aligning ourselves with change we always have the advantageous position. We work with the flow, not against it.

Better to play the game earnestly and sincerely, but without attachment to the outcome, all the while cultivating an inner spiritual satisfaction that remains unmarred by the comings and goings of the external environment. Remember, outcomes and results have their causes. If we are dissatisfied with our current outcomes we need to examine the causes within our own thought processes. If you are energizing for a particular goal, yet the outcome is unsatisfactory, then try another way, without criticizing yourself. Alter or modify your course if needed, but continue to energize in the appropriate direction and hold a vibrational consistency within your mind until the desired result appears. Success may be said to be "the ability to take consistent action." But let's examine the idea a little further.

THE MEANING OF SUCCESS

To me, success means the ability to appreciate life for what it is at present. In effect it is a form of gratitude. In reality, we have only the present moment, the past and future being only concepts that frame the all-important present. The present is our point of power, and appreciation and gratitude are remarkable allies on the way to cultivating a self-contented mind, in the present moment.

From this staging platform of gratitude we can begin to mentally construct our own personal vision of inner and outer abundance. We begin to consciously alter our vibrational consistency and when we begin to visualize abundance in our consciousness in the present tense with great emotional congruency and gratitude we set in motion the powerful process of attracting that abundance to our personal and business relationships in more tangible forms.

It's important to feel the abundance and prosperity now, in the present, because if we put ourselves mentally in the space of not having and wanting, we disempower the process. We need to start by thinking, acting and living in more prosperous ways now, in this present moment. Acting as if we are more prosperous. If you raise your internal energy in this way you will soon begin to see remarkable effects.

I used to think I couldn't afford to go out to dinner with my wife until I thought, "Why am I working so hard? What's the point if I can't even enjoy a dinner out." Then I began to think that it's important to stretch my boundary and stop thinking from limiting ideas. I then realized that, I couldn't afford *not* to go out to dinner. I owe it to myself and my family to enjoy life, not fear it, or miserly measure it with self-restricting and limiting attitudes like the fear that there won't be enough money to pay my bills.

Ultimately I believe true success is the harmony of satisfying and loving relationships with other human beings. Material wealth and prosperity can appear as a symptom of this harmony and affection, though it is not the actual source of abundant satisfaction. This type of deep clarity energizes you towards more abundant and satisfying outcomes. If love, gratitude, compassion and optimism are at the core of your being, I guarantee you will feel abundant and prosperous in ways you never could have imagined.

Once a friend told me, *"Worrying is like praying for what you don't want."* It's a form of energizing and visualizing, but in a negative and disempowering way. If we are discontented in the present, only hoping for a better future, we will be disempowering our vibrational consistency. When the future actually becomes the present moment we may still be maintaining the habitual consciousness of dissatisfaction in that "future present moment," denying us the satisfaction borne of gratitude for this present moment. So the present moment is a present...a gift that one gives to oneself through a more conscious present awareness. Practicing this form of daily gratitude and awareness conditions us for present moment satisfaction, which improves our relationship with ourselves, and others.

Equally important is the idea that it also prepares us for greater future satisfaction as well. Life is more beautiful, powerful and meaningful when we pay attention to it in the present moment. From this platform of vibrational consistency and abundance we attract increasing abundance to ourselves and those around us. *Now, and in the future.* Remember, the present moment is your power point. Forget the past. Work with the present. This moment is all you really have. Make the most of it by using vibrational consistency of thought and emotion coupled with consistently supportive actions to attract the energies that energize your growing consciousness of abundance. Visualization infused with emotional power and backed by consistent actions brings rapid results. If you follow this formula you will see a great transformation taking place in all areas of your life. Abundance is a state of mind. Monetary abundance is only a symptom of that state. Satisfying and fulfilling relationships are the true wealth and succulent fruit of this abundant mentality. Love and compassion are the greatest currency.

PARADIGM OF THE CONSCIOUS SELF

Action and reaction are floating on the surface of consciousness and it is a universal truth that whatever we experience, we ourselves have somewhere set in motion through the movements of our own mentalities and subsequent actions. Every effect has a cause, and it is far more efficient to deal with and manage causes than their effects. Release from this duality of cause and effect comes to one who disentangles his or her consciousness from the surface dream of material transformations. We can approach the threshold of our greatest inner assets when we ask ourselves the deepest question of all, "Who am I?" For, until I am at least partially self-realized, I will not realize or achieve a greater potential. As I stated earlier...

"In reality, I am a pure point of conscious light,
self-illumined awareness without beginning or end.
I am unlimited in my conscious potentiality.
It is my nature to grow and to love."

It is the conscious self that is the shining sun above and behind these processes of thought and emotion, which illuminates perception with its ever-radiant presence. Just as the sun in the sky makes all things visually perceivable, the conscious self behind the sense organs and the mind makes all physical reality perceivable.

For most of us the physical body appears to be a singular event, but in reality is a long continuum of energetic bodies...each body and mind producing the effect of the next, one after another... like a river of material manifestation flowing through time, changing, growing, morphing from this species to that sex, to this planet to that...*ad infinitum.* Whatever your particular religious orientation is, try to suspend your judgment for a moment and objectively appreciate everything from a purely energetic perspective.

Consider that we are not physical material bodies who have a soul, or consciousness. We are eternal points of consciousness having a limited physical experience...riding the waves of material energetic transformation. This is liberating knowledge and the first stage of realizing greater abundance on all levels of our life. It is backed by thousands of years of experience in the ancient cultures of the East, and substantiated by new findings in science and physics.

All the wisdom traditions of the world place greater value on the soul or consciousness than on the temporary physical body. Life is, on a deeper level, a spiritual journey and the body is a tool of manifestation. The subjective growth of the inner conscious individual is the real point of existence. The Bible says: *"Seek ye first the kingdom of God and all else shall be added unto you."* In other words, search your heart, grow your soul and expand your mind. If you make that your ultimate goal, you'll get everything else you need along the way.

Abundance will naturally follow in the wake of your unfolding inner progress if you have your priorities straight. It's a matter of substance over form. Grow your inner garden and your outer life will be benefited as well. Jesus said, *"I come that you might have life, and life more abundantly."* Clarity of spirit lets your inner light shine more brightly.

Contact with your inner nature of conscious brilliance will enhance the brilliance of your personal vitality, strength, intelligence, mind, relations, family and wealth. All will become brighter when your inner spiritual core is brighter. The purpose of our lives is to grow, and the purpose of consciousness is to expand and grow brighter. You can brighten yourself daily, through prayer, self-giving and generosity. By wishing well for others and silently blessing everyone you meet, by being kind, compassionate and non-violent, as well as by practicing yoga, meditation, puja and kirtan.

DAILY PRACTICE FOR INNER BRIGHTNESS

Generally our culture emphasizes outer directed actions for the fulfillment of desire and the advancement of position in this world. Yet these activities are often physically and mentally depleting. Everyone knows that physical exercise is good for you, but what about inner body building?

Everyday we are exposed to unhealthy toxins and sometimes we have bad eating habits that tempt us to ingest unhealthy processed foods. Also our hearts and minds are often overburdened by afflicted emotions and negative states of thinking.

For optimum satisfaction, health and prosperity, its very beneficial to practice a daily regimen of inner cleansing, nourishing and rejuvenation of the physical mental and emotional levels. According to one's temperament, faith, insight and general karmic qualities an individual will be drawn to a particular practice or faith system.

Yoga, pranayama breathing, mantra meditation, and insight practices can have a profound effect on our health and well being because they enhance our inner core energies, the subtlest aspects of our being. In Ayurveda there is the understanding of *Ojas*, or core vitality which is intimately linked to biological immunity. *Ojas* strengthens our core immunity, gives us brightness, courage, insight and intelligence. It awakens compassion, altruism and the impulse towards an awakened and enlightened mode of living.

We increase our *Ojas* when we pray, consciously breathe, meditate, chant, say grace, bless and offer our food up in gratitude and avoid negative actions such as harming others, speaking harshly and projecting negativity upon others and searching for their faults.

Compassionate and virtuous deeds that benefit others and alleviate their suffering also benefit us in many ways by leaving positive and joyful impressions upon our minds.

Take some time every morning and evening to check in with yourself. Examine your thoughts, words & deeds. Pray, visualize and make offerings to the various enlightened deities and teachers who's insights have benefited humanity. They represent ideals of human spiritual perfection. As we remember them, practice and assimilate their wisdom, our inner being brightens and is eventually transformed into a likeness of that perfection.

We have precious human lives that have great advantages of health, abundance and free time. Set aside a portion of your day in the morning or evening to rejuvenate your spiritual core. When you become brighter, you benefit everyone around you. You were meant to shine.

MY BROTHER THE PHOENIX

If you're still skeptical about the paradigm of the conscious self and the profound distinction between the material body and the soul, then read on. Because what I'm about to tell you is a true story so incredible it gives me goose bumps every time I retell it.

Let me tell you about my brother. He was three years older and subjected me to all the torment that older brothers often do. In fact these are some of the most endearing memories I have...like the time he and his friends tied me to a stop sign, stuck raisins up my nose and mercilessly tickled me for a half an hour! I had my ways of getting him back too. Like taking his Beatles 45's and flinging them as "frisbees", or putting cat pooh in his baseball mitt! Little brother revenge! Ah, those were the days!

It came as a shock to me when he suddenly passed away in 1990. Although I had half-expected it because his life had become challenged by alcohol, and the complications that accompany its abuse. But in retrospect, he taught me more than he could have guessed about life, death and myself. Our Western culture is selectively myopic about the topic of death. Perhaps we're even in denial. Ours is a culture that celebrates youth. A cult of material enjoyment that is only paused momentarily by the passing of a friend or a loved one, but then resumes full-bore it's mad pace in the pursuit of this or that and the constant distraction of the senses. We watch huge amounts of violent films yet few have ever seen a real dead body. Death is whisked away, burned and hidden from our view in the West. We don't like to see its reality, but we seem to delight in its media portrayals.

John Lennon once wisely said; *"Life is what happens when we're busy doing other things."* The same could be said about death.

Western materialistic culture often views death as an end, or the after-life as a ridiculously stereotyped heaven-fantasy. Many Asian cultures believe that in the after-life we experience the results of our actions in this life. If you've contributed to the happiness of others, you will experience a correspondingly blissful state. If you have harmed others you will encounter a correspondingly painful experience. As you sow, so you reap. Personally, that makes sense to me, and is supported by our experiences in this life.

Asian Cultures tend to view life and death as an endlessly revolving continuum as we see in nature, a cyclical play of manifest and un-manifest, a coming and going of equal value, an ebb and flow of the dynamic forces of night and day, this and that, personal consciousness and material manifestation dancing in an endless round of coming and going.

When my brother passed to the subtle realm I was deeply saddened that his life ended at such a young age but simultaneously relieved that he was released from his difficult life. I prepared his body for cremation with *tilak* (sacred clay from India) Ganges water and flower garlands from a local temple. Appropriate prayers were recited and funeral rites were duly observed. His body was cremated and I took his ashes to India to a very holy place on the Ganges River where the priests performed a *shraddha* or funeral ceremony. As I released his ashes into the holy river with prayers, many *sadhus*, or local saints were fed in his name.

That night I had the most miraculous dream. It was the most powerful and emotionally charged dream of my life. My brother appeared to me in a brilliant shining form, literally pealing rays of light from his radiant form as he hugged me saying; "thank you ...thank you. I love you brother"...I was completely melted in overwhelming emotion, tears streaming from my eyes, I woke up with a start, hyperventilating and shaking.

I was joyfully overwhelmed by the emotional impact of the experience, and ran to tell my spiritual teacher Srila Govinda Maharaja of the experience. He smiled wisely, and acknowledged; *"These things are real."* That one powerful experience of my brother's conscious evolution released me from any doubt or reservations concerning the continuation of life beyond the physical form. It was my brother's final gift to me. It was his parting gift to me of true spiritual experience that I'll always be grateful for. Perhaps some of you have had a similar profound experience with a loved one who's passed away. The scriptures of the world's greatest faiths all testify to this truth of consciousness preceding birth and continuing beyond the physical death. These truths are referred to in the Bible, the Koran and especially the *Bhagavad-gita,* India's classic treatise on dharma, devotion, and the immortality of the soul.

If we accept this deeper and profoundly simplified paradigm of the conscious non-material self, we open ourselves to a virtually unlimited potentiality. For in this idea we will find that our inner nature, at its most fundamental level, is constituted of unassailable existence, sentience, and joy. Yes, joyfulness is our natural condition at the deepest level. Non-material consciousness has immense potentiality. Just consider your dreams at night. You exist in dreams as a conscious observer with unlimited imaginative potential for miraculous growth and profound experience.

WE ARE ALL TRAVELERS

A person whose life vision is limited to this one fleeting incarnation is like the plow horse that views its life work as a single furrow, never able to appreciate how one furrow blends with the many others.

Through daily practice one gains a broader vision spanning many recurrent lives. As understanding grows, the narrow prospect of one life is detonated, the walls come tumbling down and gradually everything begins to makes sense. It's like being relieved of the misapprehension that one day is not an entire lifetime after all.

Human existence is much grander and far vaster, and invested with greater meaning than one could possibly imagine.

In extending one's understanding of life to a great succession of many lives, knowledge of reincarnation imparts significance to each existence, just as a lifetime of personal growth and achievement counts on each day's incremental contribution. Hope charged with faith accompanies this broader growing vision. Not naïve, idealistic hope, but hope founded on a mature blending of optimistic faith and scientific reason. Even the most tragic, sordid deaths can be seen to be just so many more births in the making, and that ultimately nothing can ever happen on the soul's myriad journeys except opportunities for each of us to learn and grow. There are no stagnant positions of eternal damnation. The greater energy of Divinity is a loving teacher, not a tyrant. Dynamic eternal evolution is the prospect and unconditional love is the process.

By this deeper understanding of life, every event becomes charged with higher meaning. Each thought, word and deed is rich with purpose as it bears the causes of effects to come. This brings home the truth that we are thoroughly responsible and accountable for who we are and what we do. We can no longer afford to blame circumstances or external forces of any kind for our lot in life. We are the authors of our own experience — yesterday, today and tomorrow.

A surface reading of the environment would suggest that prosperous criminals and poverty stricken saints are enduring a lack of justice in the world. Yet, none are wholly good or forever evil. The true balance and its accompanying justice are understood by the knowledge of a great succession of lives. Only through many lives of happiness and distress can the apparent inequalities of life be balanced, justified, rectified and purified.

When the individual begins to understand that he or she has personally generated every action and reaction along the way, misconceptions like "coincidence", "accident", and "inequality" lose their impact and meaning. One gains a deeper sense of understanding and freedom. We are not the prisoners of circumstance, but the makers of it.

Each of us is participating in an ultimately joyous long-range progression of self-realization spanning incalculable numbers of embodiments. In each life, a sense of incompleteness instills a continued craving for experience, which keeps bringing us back until our potential is fulfilled in spiritual perfection.

Destinies of individuals merge and interact with the collective destinies of families, communities and groups of like-minded people, nations and planets.

All are growing towards a greater understanding.
It is knowledge to know this...it is wisdom to live it.

LEVELS OF IDENTITY

As humanity moves towards a greater state of globalization the limitations of racial, gender and national identity are giving way to a higher understanding of deeper identity.

Identity is like our most essential energetic base-camp. The place you operate from determines to a large degree your range of vision and corresponding possibilities. What you identify yourself with will determine your range and reach. All of us operate on several levels of identity everyday. Recognizing these levels and understanding their corresponding assets and limitations is another tool you can use to contribute towards a more balanced and abundant life for yourself and others.

At the most basic level we have the identity as biological mammals upon the physical earth. This level is concerned primarily with survival, and views ones own selfish needs as primary. It's a very limited but concentrated view but has great power when circumstances require it.

The second level of identity is related to gender. We identify ourselves as either male or female. When this level predominates there tends to be a bias towards our own gender as in the case of exaggerated male chauvinism or its counterpart, radical feminism. Both can be equally harmful, for men and women are naturally part of one whole human experience. Honoring each other we honor our relationship and mutual growth. In the past several decades, alternate sexual orientations have also come to be recognized with corresponding ideologies and politics. Some people find this objectionable. Unconditional love and respect for others may be hard to practice in our everyday lives but its wisdom is apparent, for when we suspend our critical judgment of other peoples choices we give rise to our greater appreciation of humanity as a whole. We foster growth, for ourselves, and others. Lighten up on other people and their choices and you'll see your own life lighten and brighten as well.

The third level pertains to our racial and national identities as Europeans, Asians, Caucasian-Americans, Afro-Americans, Native-Americans, Hispanics and so on. Racial identities are also linked to our biological traits, but like gender, are also adopted, rejected or modified according to psychology and circumstance. For instance, we are all aware of how urban white kids will adopt the dress, language, attitudes and music characteristic of Afro-Americans or Rastafarians. In these days of globalization and world internet access, people from all over the world continue to blend culture, music and views that give rise to many mixtures of racial and national orientation and a healthy overview of all of these varied options.

In former times, when races and nations were more clearly defined, racial prejudice was often a national trait as in the European mood of colonial superiority towards indigenous cultures. Psychologically, this could be understood as the repression and projection of the shadow archetype by white Christian European males upon dark skinned indigenous non-Christian peoples, who's only crime was that they were the object of disdain by unsympathetic and exploitive colonial powers. The colonials feared and repressed their own wild, natural and pagan traits and as a result punished other peoples as a twisted way of trying to exorcise the savage nature in themselves, all this, with tragic consequences. Sadly, much of this racial and national bias remains and continues to foster discord between races and nations. It is a form of human ignorance that does great harm to our growth and understanding. What we negatively repress and fail to admit about ourselves, we often project upon others. Fortunately the burgeoning global economy, the global ecological crisis and the unification through technology and commerce as well as the ease of communication through the Internet, are fueling new awareness of our global humanity. This is helping to break down the former prejudices of racial stereotyping and nationalism. Yet we as human beings continue to tragically view the environment as something disconnected from ourselves and as something "other" to be exploited. It is one of the hidden factors contributing to our continuing discord by feeding exploitive competition for dwindling resources.

We can see that the first three levels of identity are strongly linked to physical and biological identification and as a result have corresponding limiting effects. If we humans are to make rapid advances in our stewardship of the planet and save ourselves and indeed, save all life forms from imminent destruction, we will need to operate our daily lives from the higher view of the conscious self, beyond biological, gender, racial, national and even human limitations.

We can make great strides in returning our societies and peoples to a natural harmony with the environment by revolutionizing our thinking from exploitation to dedication and recognizing ourselves not as the directors and dominators of nature but as conscious participants living in harmony with nature. We are only one aspect of the great wheel of life.

Technological progress can continue but must be supportive of life, and that means all life on the planet. We have to respect the environment, as a reflection of the nature of our own quality of consciousness and this "Deep Ecology" must have its roots in our deeper identities as conscious self-directed beings adopting forms and environments as tools for the inner evolution of the individual. This type of thinking will nourish the planet, rather than destroy it. When we put dedication over exploitation in our lives there is a wholesale paradigm shift for greater abundance.

On the deepest level, identity is synonymous with consciousness, and our environment always reflects our consciousness. You, me, and everyone else are unlimited in conscious potentiality. We have the power of choice, and that is our greatest freedom, our greatest power.

Advance your inner growth as a thoughtful self-directed conscious individual who respects the environment as an extension of his or her own thought processes. Live in gratitude, and respect this relationship as a sacred circle of life and a path of inner growth, a path of dedication not exploitation. Realize that everyone's inner growth is a personal and subjective experience and that we garner respect for our own choices by honoring the choices of others, even if they tend to be different or contradict our own at present. Dedication to, and respect for the wellbeing of others, unifies all life and promotes harmony on the individual, societal and global levels. Growth is the purpose of life, and when we grow internally everyone benefits.

CONSCIOUS CONTINUITY

There is a type of consciousness that arises when one practices present moment awareness. By holding one's awareness in the present through the aid of mantra repetition, prayer, internal visualizations or spacious contemplative awareness, one begins to gain a greater continuity of consciousness. This continuity of focused awareness is a great asset and power source for anyone seeking a more abundant and fulfilling life. Think of it as your own personal laser beam, like a light saber that can cut through any obstacle in your path. The present moment is your unique power point; your focus is the penetrating ability of your awareness.

Continuity of consciousness can be also maintained through the various stages of sleep and dreaming, and as the yogic traditions affirm, continuity can also be maintained even beyond the dissolution of the physical body.

When falling asleep, the conscious awareness of the waking state collapses into itself, and the life airs, *chi* or *prana,* are withdrawn from the ten senses to the energetic heart center. Upon waking we often feel a weakness in our limbs until the *prana,* or *chi* again circulates out.

When we lose conscious awareness and fall asleep, or fall into unconsciousness, there is a period of un-awareness until dream images begin to arise. The Tibetans call this the transitional *bardo,* or in-between state.

Some of these arising dream images are based upon our daily experiences and may be considered "day residue" which percolate into jumbled dream sequences of a pleasing or unpleasant nature. There is another class of impressions that may have their origin in the totality of our experience, and perhaps in previous existences as well. This greater record of experience may remain as subtle *karmic* traces that only arise when secondary causes become favorable, either in dream or in the waking states. According to Hindu and Buddhist thought, both the dreaming and waking states of consciousness are ultimately due to the karmic obscurations or subtle occlusions of misidentified conceptualizations called *samsara,* or illusory existence.

The practice of present moment awareness in the day can sometimes be carried over into the dream state, enabling one to experience lucidity within the dream.

In effect you wake up within the dream and realize that "*I am dreaming.*" This experience is often accompanied by a great exhilaration, for its accompanying realization of almost infinite possibility heightens one's experience of states and activities that transcend what is normally possible in our daily experience. The Tibetans teach that it is possible to begin manifesting conscious control of dreams. In effect, you can control the context and content of your dream states.

One can learn to fly in the sky, manifest a light body, travel to distant places, transform fire into water, and manifest celestial environments, forests and fields of magnificent beauty. Through the use of imagination you can experience all the wonders of unbridled conscious creativity, for our awareness is said to be as much as seven times enhanced in dream states.

Because our inner nature is one of subtle conscious fluidity one can more efficiently perform many types of activities in dreams, unencumbered by physical limitations. For the subtle realm is far more flexible than the gross material experience of our waking hours.

The reason why I'm sharing these ideas about lucid dreaming with you is that besides these imaginative abilities that can be developed in dreams, there is a greater potentiality to utilize these experiences to realize the transient nature of all phenomena and to carry this awareness and its transformative power back over into the waking hours of our daily life. Accompanying this realization is the further understanding of the fluidity of all forms of consciousness and the realization that our only limitations are those that we impose upon ourselves through attachment, aversion, fear and ignorance of the unlimited potentiality of our inner imaginative and spiritually conscious nature.

By bringing the understanding of the flexibility of dreams into your daily waking life, you will begin to understand that this waking life also has the miraculous potentiality of night dreams. You can intentionally use the power of consciousness and imagination in daily life just as you use it unconsciously in dreams and achieve far greater abundant results in daily life than you previously conceived possible.

Through scientific experiments and human experience it has been observed that the human nervous system cannot tell the difference between "real" and imagined experience. Athletes and musicians are famous for using this principle to train and develop skills, especially if they have been injured. If you congruently and emotionally imagine positive outcomes and activities you will begin to live and experience them in your daily life. Repetition brings skill, and skill grows greater confidence.

Again, the quality of the material objective "reality" that we are experiencing in our daily lives is a product of our own consciousness. The objective can cause effect in the subjective, but it is the subjective consciousness within us that in reality produces the objective experiences of our daily lives. Life comes from life. Inner states produce outer effects. Subtle causes give rise to gross effects. Mind ultimately produces and effects matter. Transient material phenomena manifests and floats on the surface of eternal consciousness. You grow from the inside out. This is the subjective evolution of consciousness.

The gross misidentification of self, misaligned with biological, and fabricated religious, national and racial identities can greatly minimize our potential for growth and abundance both materially and spiritually because those identities that are based on material limitations will tend to unconsciously constrict our views of what is possible. We have to learn to grow beyond the limitations of our current circumstances if we are to experience a more expansive abundant life. Believing is achieving. Ideas are the first causes. This is a fundamental principle of conscious evolution.

Reclaim your personal power in the infinite potentiality of your own spiritually conscious nature. Or as I like to say, *"Permit yourself the possibility of infinite possibilities."*

Your awareness and identification as a point of conscious light, and as a potency of the larger spiritual energetic reality of Divinity and Nature will release you from the limitations of localized identity, and place you firmly on the open road of a greater abundance that is realized when you see that the only limitations there are in life are the ones that we impose upon ourselves through limited thinking and self-labeling.

CLARITY OF PERCEPTION

Empowering ourselves with the understanding of our own spiritual identity brings greater clarity to our own psychological processes and when we direct that clarity upon objective experience we gain greater depths of understanding in the various areas of our lives.

The truth of any given situation or circumstance can be ascertained through clear awareness of its underlying facts. Distractions and self-preoccupation often occlude our ability to perceive the reality of any given experience, causing us to confuse actual events with our own emotional and mental projections.

We can move beyond this mixed state when we realize that subjective psychological understandings hold an intermediate position in the hierarchy of conscious perception.
Spiritual insight is a higher and clearer perceptual experience that is facilitated by our conscious release from mentally conditioned states of thinking and behaving. The paradigm of the non-material self is like sunlight streaming through the clouds, it brings inspiration and shines forth upon our experience... sometimes in our most bewildering moments.

When we clearly perceive the facts of any given situation, and place our understanding before our feelings, we empower ourselves to greater and more efficient action, which in the long run is far more beneficial for everyone. Conversely, when we try to feel a fact before actually understanding its reality clearly, we may fall into error and create unnecessary disturbances through psychological projections and the drama that results from them.

As you read these words, the subtle impressions of the characters enter through your eyes, which along with the skin, nose, ears and mouth, is one of the sense organs of perception. The impression of printed word is transmitted neurally from the initial impression upon the optic nerves to the brain. The brain is the physical instrument that houses the subjective experience of the subtle mind.

Mind is the cognitive repository of all of these perceptual impressions or psychic-sensory-traces, and the intelligence is the discriminatory feature that deliberates over the dualism of these impressions. The mind is also the penumbra of the ever-illumined conscious self, just as radiance surrounds a flame.

It is the conscious self that is the shinning sun above and behind all of these processes. The self is that which illuminates perception with its ever-radiant conscious presence. Just as the sun in the sky makes all things visually perceivable, the conscious self behind the sense organs and the mind makes all physical reality perceivable. Consciousness and physical manifestation are co-dependent, and ever influencing one another in an endless dynamic loop of idea, manifestation, perception and experience, leading to new ideas.

Our thoughts create our actions, which create our behaviors, which forms our character, which effects our perceptions, which conditions our thoughts. The paradigm of the non-material conscious self allows you the ability to raise your awareness to a greater height, which affords a broader perspective of these energetic processes, which in turn leads to a greater sense of mastery of your inner psychological and emotional processes.

Armed with this knowledge, you can detach yourself from the inner quagmire of conflicting emotional states and begin to enjoy the abundant power and freedom that comes from a more clearly defined spiritual identification. As Vernon Howard once said, *"If you're not the person you think you are, you don't have the problems you think you do."*

This inner clarity cleanses the doors of perception, which are the gateways of energetic flow in your more abundant and satisfying life.

CLARITY OF PURPOSE

Sometimes I have to ask myself....."what is my *raison d'etre,* my purpose in life?" Generally we think in terms of what can be gained, but really, it's about what we can contribute or give to life. The Hindus call it *dharma*...one's sacred duty or more succinctly, our innermost quality and expression. I believe this is love, unconditional love, and on a spiritual level the unconditional love of an individual soul for its Sacred Source...the All-love or Divinity. This is the deepest dharma for everyone. In India it's called *sanatan-dharma,* meaning the eternal occupation of the soul. In our everyday life we can harmonize more fully with the energetic abundant flow of the universe by identifying our own dharma or life purpose. It affords us a greater emotional congruency and inner focus of idealized visualization that acts as the magnet for greater abundant flow to you. For all of us, no matter who we are, growth and greater realization is the ultimate purpose of life, and that growth comes most powerfully through self-giving, loving kindness, and contributing to the welfare of all living beings.

Material acquisition is fine but it can never satisfy the appetite for material acquisition. It is like trying to grasp a flowing stream of water through one's hands. Only self-realization and the lasting contentment it affords can satiate our desires once and for all.

A wisdom paradigm of abundant living and giving, coupled with vibrational consistency and congruent action is a greater dynamic of self-contented yet active abundance. It is a dynamic fullness that does not need to be constantly fed from outside, for it is fed by the underground wellspring of inner reality.

Giving is getting in disguise, and this becomes more clearly realized when the bigger absolute picture of the circle of life comes into view.

If we want more of anything in our life we will have to give more. If it's more money that we want, we will have to invest more consciousness, more time and more action. People who operate at higher financial levels of success are doing so because they are contributing more of their personal energy towards that outcome. So if you want more financial success in your life it means that you will have to give more of yourself to achieve that. Results don't lie. So at this point you really have to ask yourself, "What do I really want?" Most of us will say yes I'd like more money, but few of us are willing to enter that busier circle of energetic give and take...or flow, as I like to call it.

But working harder is not the answer, working smarter is.

Money magnifies our situations and emotions. If you win the lottery chances are you'll go through it quickly and may not be able to hang onto your newfound wealth unless you develop a new type of thinking regarding wealth and what it can do. Professional athletes make enormous amounts of money during their active years but less than 20% of them maintain a very high level of financial solvency beyond their last season. Winning the lotto may not do much good for you if you still live in poverty consciousness. Wealth is an inner state of abundance, a type of psychological maturity that is independent of loss and gain. Money is just an outward symbol.

Statistically, lottery winners are not happier than others. Suddenly receiving large amounts of money invariably throws their lives into chaos, leading to divorce, conflict and sometimes bankruptcy. I know a twenty-something girl who received a great inheritance of $600,000. Her sudden wealth attracted several men into her life who preyed upon her generosity and lack of financial understanding. She was exploited by people who drained away all her wealth. Within two years she was back in Oregon living in the woods in a shack with no electricity, no property and barely enough gas money to drive into town. Wealth came, but she was unable to keep it, because she lacked clarity, purpose and inner direction.

If you want to enter a higher financial experience you will first need to grow into the person who can handle it, and besides, the best part of becoming wealthier is the inner growth process it takes to reach that higher financial level. The green stuff is just an outer symbol of the inner growth and transformation. So carefully choose your goals and then clarify them, but most of all put a spiritual ideal at the center, like helping others, improving conditions or contributing to the greater harmony of the world at large. In other words, make your goal a force for good, and it will transform you into goodness as well. Keep yourself in the flow and the flow will be with you. Life will support your ideal if it's generous.

Energetically speaking, we all have a role to play and we have been drawn to this life to act out a particular pattern of actions that are the results of our current vibrational consistency as well as past energetic contributions. The important thing is to connect with the life purpose that most deeply resonates with your heart. For some that may be teaching, nourishing or protecting. Some are called to artistic and musical contributions, others will cultivate the land or build. Whoever you are, you have a purpose and a contribution to make. By gaining clarity of purpose you will add another key component to achieving a more satisfying and abundant life that will nourish your own inner growth and outer abundance, as well as contribute to the greater good of others.

Participation in the flow of abundance with clarity of purpose, without a grasping identification, empowers our aesthetic appreciation, awakening our sense of profound wonder and appreciation for the magnificent beauty of all things spiritual and mundane. This life is a play of energies and we can play with a lighter and more joyful spirit when we have a deeper understanding of the dynamics involved supporting our clarity. Everywhere we witness the ever-changing patterns of nature. The wonderful dance of life, and the revolutions of the stars and planets, the changes of the seasons, years, months, days and hours. Within each moment is a micro-revolution of amazing proportions if we had but the perceptual equipment to perceive it.

Yet each moment is really but a measurement of our own consciousness, for time is a construct of the materially occluded. Actually there is only now. Often we suffer from the past and generate anxiety or apprehension regarding possible future events, yet the whole show is actually going on behind our own eyes.

Like walking projectors, we project outward the qualities that are the constituents of our own inner paradigm, for better or worse. Disharmony ensues when we dance out of step with our own life purpose. With impartial awareness we are afforded a glimpse of the way things truly are, not as we misrepresent them in relation to our own misidentification with temporal

53

manifestations. This is clarity at a deeper level. In clarifying our life purpose, we find the power of authenticity and abundance of opportunity in regard to the manifestation of our own unique contribution. It unifies us. The Native Americans have a saying *"No tree has branches so foolish as to argue amongst themselves."* When we unite our inner psychology for our greater good, we empower ourselves more than any external force ever could. Jesus said: *"If thine eye be single, thy whole body shall be filled with light."* Illumination is clarity, and clarity is power.

Why do we fear that change will take things away from us? Spiritually, change is never a loss, it is only change. Competition and limitation are false measurements that deny our actual abundance in eternal consciousness where there is no limitation...only an ever-increasing abundant potentiality.

Active yet detached participation in this beautiful dance of life enriches the heart and draws us together in the unity of our own growth potential. Seek out your deepest life calling and begin to nourish the vision of yourself contributing in that role. As this inner vision grows in clarity it will energize you to greater achievements. Success in the main area of purpose can then be transferred to other secondary or peripheral areas of endeavor as well, and will assist in the nourishment of your central ideal.

CLARITY OF SOURCE

Within you flows a hidden wellspring of inspiration. If a farmer relies exclusively upon rain from the sky, he will forever be in anxiety about the changing weather conditions in the environment. His neighbor, on the other hand, who has an underground wellspring, will enjoy a carefree state of mind due to his confidence in the regular flow of nourishment from his own property. The changes in the weather will not negatively affect him as they do his neighbor.

Similarly, if we pin our hopes for happiness on other people, on future circumstances, on the objects of the senses or anything outside of ourselves, we set ourselves up for anxiety, heartbreak and disappointment. We disempower ourselves substantially and lose sight of the great power we have in our own abilities to choose and direct our states, our energies and our lives.

Within the heart of each conscious living being there is vast intelligence, wisdom, beauty, abundant and infinite potentiality, as well as the lasting spiritual satisfaction that we are all longing for. It is not foreign from our intrinsic nature as conscious spiritual beings.

Yet, we have become alienated from our own essential nature through our addiction to the objects of the senses and preoccupations with the temporal, the insubstantial illusory material phenomena. Remarkably, we put on masks and pretend to be the wise and satisfied persons that we actually are!

The divine guardian power that governs the environment is a vast inexhaustible reality of infinite potentiality and abundance. We are a potency and interdependent "part" of that infinite reality. As my teacher often said, reality is a beautiful *unity in diversity*, a symphonic and harmonious at-one-ness, and an organic holistic system of life.

The feeling of lack in our lives is actually our own lack of faith in our inseparable relation with this divine abundant reality. Our fulfillment in life is not dependent upon acquiring more objects from the environment but rather awakening our conscious relationship with this reality of infinite potentiality referred to by modern researchers as *the quantum field* and known to the world's great religious traditions as God, Goddess, and Divinity. The ancient Sanskrit-speaking yogic culture of India recognized this great spirit as Lakshmi-Vishnu, the omnipresent beautiful reality, The all-pervading and everlasting conscious witness... who's center is everywhere and who's circumference is nowhere. *Reality the Beautiful, the all-pervading transcendence.*

This quantum field, in reality is not an *"it" but a "who"* in the super-subjective conscious sense, and reveals a glimpse of its own transcendent reality to us when our necessity is great and our prayer sincere. God responds to our sincerity, and prayer is a link to our own divine nature and an act of uniting ourselves once again with the abundant flow of the universe. The plurality of religious doctrines in the world is the outcome of the plurality of sincere approaches made by those who sought deep understanding and received a corresponding insight. As that initial revelation and conception became systematized into a spiritual or religious methodology, tradition and culture, it took on a formality of structure that later would impede its originally dynamic and living quality. This is the inevitable vitiation of truth in the conditioned atmosphere of time, space and matter.

The culture and awareness of the omnipresent reality throughout life will transform us consciously from a limiting material paradigm to an ever-expanding awareness of greater abundance deeply rooted in a spiritual understanding of life. The goal of many religious practices is to gain entrance to that everlasting inexhaustible beauty at the crucial moment of death, relieving the conscious individual of the miseries of cyclical existence in material phenomena. Yet, salvation and liberation are only by products of love. If we truly and deeply love others and seek to serve the greater good of others we need not be overly concerned about our own salvation, for our growing spiritual love and concern for all beings is a greater spiritual abundance that will automatically ensure our own greater spiritual good. There's an old saying *"If you row someone across the river, you arrive there as well."*

We may have some beliefs that are no more than surface opinions without substance. Like mushrooms, their roots do not run very deep in our being for they merely float upon our mental system, and were acquired unconsciously through the osmosis of our associations with family members and peers.

Faith is not merely belief, but a very subtle trust that is rooted in our conscious being. It is an expression of our very nature as eternal conscious substance. It is the luster of the soul and is characterized as a deep abiding trust in the unseen reality of the divine sovereign guardian power of vast inexhaustible and infinite potentiality and abundance.

Faith and clean love, characterized by selfless service, are our connection with the universal flow of the omnipresent reality. You can consciously enter that flow and realize your wealth in your active love and concern for others.

That reality is within you. It is your potent source of greater abundance. It need only be uncovered through vibrational consistency, selfless action and affection for all beings.

CLARITY OF TIME

Occasionally we encounter moments in our lives where the miraculous and deeply meaningful nature of life becomes apparent to us...yet everyday we live in that same miraculous universe, even when on the surface it may not appear so.

In those cherished moments of insight we forget the difficulties, fears and frustrations that harass and distract us...and from this perspective we can come to realize that "enlightenment" and other such states of deep insight and joy, are not something to be achieved or won through our hard work and iron-jawed will-power, ritualistic action or meditative or intellectual study...but that these exalted states are in truth a pre-existent state within us waiting to be recognized and uncovered...as they relate to the essential ground of our being in consciousness. Our inner consciousness is of the nature of that unified field of underlying infinite potentiality. At the deepest level we are success, wisdom and joy, and we can uncover this wealth in our daily lives.

Such insights of unfolding conscious awareness become apparent when our *intensity of inquiry exceeds the depth of their occlusion.* Here we may recognize the truth of the statement *"Seek and ye shall find"..."Knock, and the door shall be opened to you".* By intensity of purpose we literally penetrate the barrier of our own ignorance and uncover our own hidden treasure of immense potentiality.

Holding our awareness to the beauty of the present consolidates and concentrates our internal energies to an almost mystic precision that enables our higher cognitive faculties to penetrate, like a laser beam, even the most deeply pressing situations, circumstances and questions. The illusion of linear time denies the reality of the Unity of Now. Past and future are but shadows of the eternal *Now.* By practicing present moment awareness and concentration these deeper truths of our inner spiritual nature and unlimited potentiality come to the fore and empower us to a better today and an even brighter and greater tomorrow. If we examine all the technological marvels that we take for granted in today's world...the underlying factor in their manifestation is always concentrated observation, experimentation and consistent actions based on this awareness. In effect, intense observation, clarity and action. Isn't this the point where mysticism and science converge?

THE WEALTH OF NOW

The great 19th century theologian, Bhaktivinode Thakur once wrote:

"Forget the past that sleeps and n'er the future dream at all.
But act in times that are with thee and
progress ye shall call".

Have you ever noticed that the past and the future are mental concepts that drag our attention away from the present moment? This moment, right now is your true point of power. It's the place where everything happens. The past is gone, but the future can be pregnant with possibility if we make the investment in this present moment. If we develop the habit of mindfulness in the present, that habit will be present in our future, and through consistent practice, our concentration will increase, as well as our ability to manage our own inner environment of thought and mood.

The past has no hold upon us except that which we assign it by placing our attention upon it. If you have a troubled past, you can change the way you feel about it *now*, and significantly alter its impact upon you *now*. Most of us at one time or another wander into the past and suffer over events and people that are long gone. We also habitually fret and worry over events that have not yet come to pass. Neither one of these mental wanderings have ever done us much good yet we persist in the damaging habit of deviating from the present, where our power of choice resides.

When we indulge in the negative past and the fearful future we sap our vitality from the sweet spot where life is really happening... *now!* If you want more abundance in all areas of your life you've got to free yourself from the bad habit of living in the wrong time zone. There is no past or future in reality. There is only the eternal now. That may sound like a far-out mystical idea but it's a psychological fact. Linear time is a conceptual product of our conscious processes.

It's normal and healthy to draw from past experience as well as envision a better future but we must not dwell in either of these zones predominantly more than the present. We can more effectively envision a better future from the present moment by remaining consciously aware in the now.

Mark Twain said: *"I have been through some terrible things in my life. Some of which actually happened."*

He was referring to negative imagination and as you probably know, we often employ negative imagination in regard to both the past and the future. As I mentioned before *"Worrying is like praying for what you don't want."* It's the same process as creative visualization, just unconsciously employed to bring about a destructive result. Unfortunately we are often the victims of our own destructive thought patterns. Where we choose to place our attention determines where we go emotionally. Wherever we direct our attention, our energies will gather and increase. Take a minute and disengage your mind from reading. Concentrate on your toes. Feel them glowing and buzzing with energy. Direct all your attention there. Try it. With practice you can direct your attention and energy within your body to any location in your body. You can do the same thing with emotions. It takes some practice. As you gain experience, you will realize a new power within yourself when you consciously direct your thoughts and emotional states. It's a true and abiding power because where we go emotionally effects how we represent events to ourselves, and how we represent events to ourselves effects our physiology, health and overall well being. It's a wealth of self-mastery.

Negative thoughts and emotions can act as a loop or a carousel.

Like chasing our tail, we sometimes spin out of control emotionally or mentally, yet we ourselves give energy to these experiences by bringing them to life with our attention. You can starve the negative patterns by not allowing them the energy of your attention. This can be done by getting into the habit of moving your energy of attention to the various parts of your body. This robs the energy from the negative film loop in your head and enables you to consciously direct your inner energies.

It was a great breakthrough for me on the day when I realized that I was running a negative film in my head about *"what might happen."* It was both a blessing and a shock to realize that I was imagining negative scenarios in my mind and on top of it all, I was getting myself upset about what I was imagining! Have you ever done this? Sure you have. We all have. Crazy isn't it? It's a great moment of insight to realize how we make ourselves miserable, but it's a greater gain when we realize we have the wisdom to actually do something about it. Put an end to your own negative imaginings. You'll be surprised how pleasant your life can be when you stop upsetting yourself. You'll also realize how much precious energy you were squandering in order to unnecessarily torment yourself.

Unity and consolidation of consciousness, as well as focus and inner harmony are the cure-all for mental turbulence. Emotional difficulties arise when we are divided against ourselves. The inner contradiction creates pain for ourselves, and everyone around us. When you bring these facts up to conscious awareness you gain the power of emotional control. Like anything we practice it may take some time to become skillful, but remember, any investment in your self brings a 100% return. Progress in self-understanding is always beneficial.

When you stand on a mountaintop you can see everything clearly below. Self-awareness, clarity and simplicity are like climbing a holy mountain in your heart. As we climb higher in self-understanding, everything seems clearer, fresher and simpler. We have a saying in the sign business, *"The closer to heaven, the more forgiveness there is."* In other words, the higher your perspective, the better your quality of life.

Focusing on the present moment and consciously remaining present in the Now brings both inner and outer events into clearer perspective and can free us from the habitual tendency to allow the mind to run wild through jungles of convoluted negative imaginations.

View each thought and emotion as they pass, if they are related to a past event or future imagination, remain consciously present in the *now* and allow them to pass, as you would allow a ship to pass on the sea or a cloud slowly passing across a clear blue sky.This sort of inner detachment keeps us centered, and when we are centered in the present we make clearer and more beneficial choices.

Unnecessary and negative comparisons to others may occasionally divert our attention but a healthy understanding of our individual uniqueness and self-worth brings up a greater wealth of self-appreciation from the depths of our hearts out upon the energetic stage of our daily life. You will treat others as you treat yourself, and as you treat yourself with more understanding and self-acceptance you will become more compassionate towards others as well.

RELEASE FROM NEGATIVITY

Occasionally, when the light of clarity is cast upon our inner processes, the shadows grow long as well. When this happens we should not curse the light, but understand that clarity and awareness includes the perception of the shadow sides of consciousness. If we observe the occasional emergence of negativity within our thinking processes, we can disarm it rapidly by the process of self-releasing. This is done first by observing its presence and secondly by not allowing oneself to become emotionally involved with the negative pattern. If you begin to wrestle with it, you engage it with your attention and it will grow stronger from your attention. You can think of it as a dark cloud passing through the sky of your mind...allow it to pass.....*release it*...see your inner awareness as a shining sun and emotionally and cognitively disengage yourself from the cloud of passing negativity and consciously allow it to pass. Let it go. Let it be... and rest in the radiance of your own intrinsic awareness.

DON'T LABEL THE EXPERIENCE

Generally, when we have any type of experience our inner tendency is to measure it in terms of good or bad. Which means we label it in some way or other. When we label experience, we will then emotionally respond to our label, which ties us in to a particular set of experiences of limited range. We limit ourselves as soon as we label and prematurely foreclose the creative possibility of any given experience. By labeling experiences we also engage them and energize them.

The most effective way to approach any situation with optimal clarity is to emotionally detach yourself from the experience. *If you don't identify yourself with the experience or the labeling of it, you will be free of any negative emotional response to it.* Remain neutral. Don't personalize the experience. Don't label or negatively judge the situation but remain creatively and lightly aware through the changes. It's a bit like mental surfing. You ride the wave without being emotionally submerged by it.

Your focus on the creative potential in any given situation elevates your aesthetic appreciation while simultaneously freeing you from the entangling bramble patch of negative emotional attachment and involvement. Trust me, it's a far more elegant way to move through the world and will empower you to greater possibility and appreciation of the inherent beauty and abundance to be discovered in each daily event.

The purpose of life is to grow, expand, realize and nourish ourselves as well as everyone around us. We can grow from any position. Just as a beautiful lotus flower may grow from healthy soil or a muddy pond. Our attention is the watering process. By cultivating the understanding that we are miraculous, wonderful and beautiful, we energize ourselves, and others, to a far higher unique potentiality of experience on all levels. Give yourself permission to transcend the internalized negativities, judgments, and malevolent "authority" of the past. Try to realize that in this moment you are unique, beautiful and free.

Permit yourself the possibility of infinite possibilities.

THE ABUNDANCE INDUCTION TECHNIQUE

Thank you for staying with me and reading this far. Perhaps many of these ideas are familiar to you, others may not be, but your active participation in reading, absorbing, acting out, and realizing these ideas and concepts is abundant evidence of a willingness to grow and change and heralds an increasingly abundant flow in all areas of your life. Idea is the primitive form of attainment, and just reading and thinking about these ideas means that you are increasing your participation in the abundant flow of life. You are stepping into a new view of your own energetic possibilities.

Now I'd like to share with you a powerful meditative technique that you can use on a daily basis to increase awareness and abundant energy flow. It involves several techniques that help you make dramatic shifts in your consciousness and once you understand the basic formula you can use this technique to improve your abundance in all areas of your life. But first let me give you a little background information.

In our realization of an increasingly abundant life it's necessary to have a general understanding of the unconscious mind and align ourselves in harmony with this powerful inner resource. You see, most of us live in such a way that our unconscious minds often work against us instead of supporting our positive growth. The unconscious mind itself is neutral and is not to be blamed. It will produce results regardless of the type of content you supply, so our next step is to begin supplying positive and abundant ideas that support our growth in abundant consciousness.

One definition of the unconscious mind is that it is that hidden part of the mind which gives rise to a collection of mental phenomena that manifest in a person's mind but which the person may not be aware of at the time of their occurrence. These phenomena include unconscious feelings, unconscious or automatic skills, unnoticed perceptions, unconscious thoughts, unconscious habits and automatic reactions, psychological complexes, hidden phobias and concealed desires.

The unconscious mind can be seen as the source of night dreams and automatic thoughts that appear without apparent cause. The unconscious is also the repository of memories that have been forgotten, but remain emotionally charged, like hidden land mines, forgotten, but still live. These memory states may be linked to certain stimuli that trigger corresponding emotional responses. The unconscious mind is also the center of implicit knowledge, or all the things that we have learned so well that we do them without thinking. One familiar example of the operation of the unconscious is the phenomenon where one fails to immediately solve a given problem and then suddenly has a flash of insight that provides a solution perhaps days later at some odd moment during the day or within dreams.

So the basic idea is that we will be introducing new, more

accurate and positive material into the unconscious mind, but just how this is done makes all the difference! This technique I'm about to share with you goes beyond common affirmations because it involves a self-hypnotic methodology that bypasses the critical factor of the mind and powerfully induces a state of greater receptivity to abundance on the deepest levels of the unconscious mind. If you follow this method and work with this technique you will begin to realize greater abundance in your personal and financial affairs by aligning yourself with the great power of the unconscious mind.

As most of us know, an affirmation is a carefully formatted statement that is repeated to one's self and written down frequently. For an affirmation to be effective, it needs to be present tense, positive, personal and specific. However, the problem with affirmations is that if they are practiced without bypassing the critical factor of the mind, they can often inadvertently program the unconscious to deliver the opposite of the desired outcome. You see, when we try not to think of something we have already unconsciously set that very thing up in our unconscious mind as the goal. Which produces the opposite effect. If I say to myself *"I don't want to be poor,"* the unconscious mind hears the word poor and carries that idea as well as all of the associated ideas connected with poverty into our experience. We are in effect telling the unconscious mind that we are poor. The correct and efficient way to approach this situation would be to reframe the affirmation as *"I am growing more prosperous everyday."* However, even this positively expressed affirmation can be rendered ineffective if the background voice of the mind's critical factor is not relaxed because it will subtly imply that because I'm repeating the positive affirmation I'm unconsciously and simultaneously allowing its opposite concept to arise, which is that *"I'm only aspiring for increasing wealth because I don't have it today."* This may seem like ridiculous hair-splitting semantics, but the mind is very subtle, and the unconscious subtler still, and to gain greater effectiveness in these matters, in my humble opinion, bypassing the critical factor is essential because it effectively releases us from the duality of cognitive associations that naturally arise in the practice of affirmations and positive thinking.

HOW IT WORKS

Here's how the "Abundance Induction Technique" works. The best time to work with this technique is just before bedtime and immediately upon waking. At these critical junctures of waking and sleeping we are in a far more receptive condition than at other times of day when the critical factor of the mind is highly active.

Besides the fact that early morning is generally a very quiet time and is ideal for meditative states, the imagination is also greatly enhanced in these quiet hours and can be directed in such a way as to powerfully influence the unconscious mind. You know that warm comfortable feeling you have of partial conscious awareness just as you emerge from sleep. Its called the hypnogogic state. It's a time of great receptivity for the unconscious mind and the ideal time to induce a self-hypnotic state and effectively introduce beneficial content to the unconscious mind.

As you lay there in bed, you can begin to visualize your body as a field of light. From the heart region envision a beautiful warm light radiating out into all of your limbs and as it radiates out from the center of your being it pushes out of your fingertips and toes all tension and negativity that you may also envision as darkness. Just let all darkness and tension flow effortlessly out from your fingertips and toes until your whole being is filled with a comfortable radiant light that increases with every breath.

With every breath feel and see the light growing brighter within you, bringing with it greater contentment and relaxation. Your body feels lighter and brighter with each breath and your physical relaxation grows to such a great extent that your body feels as if it is floating.

At this point you should be in a completely relaxed and receptive state in which critical thinking is inactive and imagination is greatly enhanced. In this enhanced state of imaginative relaxation you can begin to introduce an inner dialog with accompanying visualizations of your greater abundance. Remember, the unconscious mind cannot tell the difference between an actual physical experience and one that is vividly imagined.

Now begin creating a narrative flow of words and images using linguistic bridges that effortlessly link the narrative and images into a seamless cognitive flow of experience.

You can begin the narrative like this. "I am a being of energetic light. With every breath my brightness increases and I feel more comfortable and receptive to the goodness and abundance that surrounds me. And as I feel more deeply relaxed I experience greater abundant flow of all the energies in life. As this flow increases I realize more deeply that wealth and abundance is a dynamic flow of energy, and as this energy continues to flow I am able to release all tension in my life and clearly see that the more I give to others, the more energy and abundance flows towards me, because I am a living part of the flow of all energies and the more I give the more flows to me and as more flows away from me, more flows to me. There is no lack in the energetic and brightly flowing energy of the universe. Every wave of energy that flows to me or away from me brings me more abundantly into the flow of all abundant flow."

As you let your seamless narrative flow on in this natural and relaxed way be sure to see yourself vividly in the company of the energies you are attracting. If you are consciously trying to manifest more financial wealth you may wish to visualize large stacks of cash in your hands. If you've ever held a large stack of money remember how that feels...the weight of the money in your hands, what the bills look like as you flip through the stack... the feel of the small breeze that brushes your face as you do so, the smell of the ink on the paper. The point is to get all of your senses involved with the experience. You want to feel yourself holding the money and feel the great emotional excitement that accompanies the heightened experience of holding large amounts of money.

Remember, this isn't an exercise to increase our greed or lust for money. It's a meditation that familiarizes you with the actual feelings and experiences of being more wealthy, which is a state of abundant consciousness. Paper money, gold and other objects of great financial value are *only* symbols of this abundant state of consciousness that you are cultivating in this exercise. The real power is in the increased consciousness of energetic flow of life. The purpose is inner growth and an increased ability to share in loving exchange.

Abundant people may or may not have the outward symptoms of wealth like cars, homes and cash. But the real factor is the inner kingly state of mind. This is the expanded consciousness of abundant opportunity and energetic flow. This type of thinking will bring more of everything into your life. It could be love, better relations with others, more opportunities, actually any goal you like.

Now if you've never had the experience of holding large sums of money I encourage you to develop your familiarity with what that actually feels like because it will bring your inner experience more powerfully into the realm of tangible manifestation.

Once when I was with a wealthy friend he handed me a bag that held $50,000 dollars in cash. At that point in my life it was the most cash I'd ever held and I consciously noted the weight of it in my hands. At that moment I realized that I had unconsciously distanced myself from the experience of holding large sums. After all, most of us rarely get the opportunity to physically experience that much money in our personal presence, especially in this digital age of debit and credit cards, bank drafts etc. So it was a moment of realization to hold that much cash. I realized I had negative unconscious attitudes about money and I had emotionally distanced myself from the experience of having an abundant flow of prosperity in my life.

You see I had linked negative emotions to money because I was often upset and feeling needy when I paid my bills or when I went to the bank, and those repeated experiences reinforced the concept in my unconscious mind that money was a symbolic link to unhappy emotional states. I had grown up with a self-image of myself as often being in financial need. It was necessary for me to make peace with prosperity and end, once and for all, my love-hate relationship with money, by replacing it with a much healthier attitude of energetic flow. Not long after that I found myself in the presence of nearly $150,000 in cash and a year later over $200,000. It wasn't my money, but I found it interesting that now I began to move in circles where large sums of cash were available. Not long after that my own level of prosperity and abundance began to steadily increase with my increasing inner contentment to a better quality of life.

I believe that if you really want to experience something more tangibly you must begin by becoming more intimate with the object of your desire. Like attracts like. If you don't have access to large stacks of money you can purchase stacks of "heavenly bank notes" from some of the larger Asian markets and begin holding these simulated stacks of money until you are familiarized with what it feels like. After all, what are "real" bank notes? They are ink on paper. But the wealth is not the notes themselves but the value that resides in our consciousness. We impart value from our minds to the symbolic notes themselves. Again, wealth is subjective. It's a state of consciousness, and idea is the herald of attainment.

Consider gold. It's a naturally occurring metal, but its true value doesn't reside in the objective experience of gold, *the metal*. The real value of gold resides in our collective consciousness that has agreed to impart value to an otherwise useless soft yellow metal. Lead could just as easily be as valuable as gold if the human race decided to shift the value we ascribe to gold upon lead instead.

Practicing this abundance induction technique and familiarizing yourself with the energies that you most wish to attract into your own energetic flow will do wonders in bringing about a more clearly defined consciousness of abundance in your life. Soon after it will become a tangible reality.

Utilize your own clarity and abundance of perception, purpose, source and time. Write them down and clearly define them in your mind and feel them in your body. Clarity is power. Ideas are magnetic. Now lets talk about energetic receptivity.

CHAPTER TWO
RECEPTIVITY

"There are no fixtures in nature. The universe is fluid and volatile.
Permanence is but a word of degrees."
-Ralph Waldo Emerson

OPEN TO RECEIVE

One of my favorite authors, Vernon Howard once wrote,

"If we wish to watch or record a scheduled broadcast it is necessary to tune our television or radio appropriately. Once our equipment is properly set-up for correct reception we need do little else but relax in the confidence and knowledge that the program must eventually be ours to experience."

If we can set our inner dial to the open position and remain receptive with an open heart, that state of openness will reveal much to us that was once hidden. There is much wealth within us and around us, but our receptors are tuned incorrectly. Human beings have an amazing capacity to act as receiving units capable of intuiting higher wisdom and clearer psychological and spiritual perceptions. This is especially so when we begin to abandon the practice of broadcasting our own false projections into the environment. When we unite our natural intelligence with the true self of conscious spiritual existence, much insight is gained and our inner unity will lead us to clarity, receptivity and personal power. Flexibility of attitude is the first threshold we must pass on this inner journey and receptivity is the framework. In order for you to realize greater receptivity in your life there are two pre-requisites that dramatically clear the way. These are clarity (or freedom from confusion) and flexibility of attitude. We often resist change, and perhaps it's human nature to do so, but we can get leverage over this tendency by a greater understanding of the process and inevitability of change. Change is inevitable and inescapable. In fact, it's one of the most remarkable constants in life and if we align ourselves with its magnificent flowing power we can reap the tremendous benefits of a more abundant life in a more relaxed and elegant way. Remember, abundance is not my ability to acquire and guard anything *from* change, but rather, my realization that true abundance is linked to my inner harmony *with* change. I am surrounded at all times by immense amounts of flowing energy and information. Everything I need and desire already exists in its potential state within the conscious matrix of unlimited potentiality.

So if you're dissatisfied with your current circumstances, be glad! Because it means you're at the threshold of greater change and abundance. The Poet Rumi wrote: *"Sell your cleverness for bewilderment."* There is a great deal of crazy wisdom in these words because they acknowledge impermanence, which aligns us with uncertainty, which is where vitality resides. If we are courageous enough to ride it out, and clear enough to recognize the greater opportunities coming into view, we will be benefited in many ways.

In Chapter One, I told my story of my dissatisfaction while working in a film lab, and how that dissatisfaction was used as propulsion to seek a better opportunity. My faith in my own ability and greater worth, combined with my consistent action, brought about the dramatic life change that followed. But it was preceded by receptivity to new possibilities and the flexibility to try something new. We must develop the courage to face and pursue change, not wait for it to happen to us. You will find great personal power and beauty in your life when you realize you have the freedom to design your own life. Many play victim by giving away their power to other people and circumstances. You and I are now done with that disempowering illusion. It is the worst sort of self-betrayal. You are the author of your own experience. Believe it and take charge of yourself by observing your mental processes and learn to direct the energetic patterns within you. Your thoughts and emotions are your assistants, not your taskmasters. Receptivity to these concepts will shave years off the learning curve of your life. Learn to relax and be open to the energies of life. Read the energetic patterns in and around you in the people and the environment, and soon you will become more skillful in your dealings.

MY STORY OF RECEPTIVITY

In the spring of 1998 I was living in the Santa Cruz Mountains in the beautiful area of Ben Lomond. We had originally moved to Felton from San Mateo in 1992 and immediately fell in love with the area with its proximity to the Santa Cruz beaches and majestic primal redwood forests. I had grown up in the more urban San Mateo area which is just an hour south of San Francisco. By 1990 I could feel my life about to shift for the better.

In fact it was a year of dramatic shift. I was newly married and making good money as a graphic designer and sign installer. I had a measure of independence because I worked as an independent contractor for a large sign company in San Carlos. Sadly, that year my older brother Eric died at age 35 and that was a great emotional blow and turning point for me. It's amazing how life will sometimes give you a tough lesson through one door and open a higher window somewhere else. That window was about to open.

I had been visiting Santa Cruz since I was a child for summer beach excursions and by 1992 my visits had become more frequent. I loved to spend time by the ocean or wander through the lush forests of the Santa Cruz Mountains with several new friends who lived in that area. One day as I was complaining about living in busy San Mateo my good friend Chet offered to rent me his house in the town of Felton for $750.00

At that time I was paying $950.00 for an upstairs unit in a big Victorian house in San Mateo. The landlord, his wife and child lived below us and although they were pretty nice to us, I never liked living above my landlord and hearing his booming voice yelling at his wife and child. So when Chet offered me his sweet little one-bedroom house in the woods we eagerly accepted his offer. It meant that we would have to drive over the hill to work on the peninsula spending as much as three hours on the road a day but I felt it was worth it and I was ready for a change of scenery.

The first few years were very difficult because, although I made a good living installing signs and my wife was working for a non-profit, neither of our incomes were very consistent at that time. We were generally living a scaled down version of our former San Mateo life, though we were surrounded by natural beauty. Both of us had lived in a spiritual ashram for many years and were quite accustomed to living simply but when our son Sundar was born in 1993 we felt the need for greater economic abundance. Gradually, over the next few years, I began to establish my economic base in Santa Cruz, thus eliminating the need for the long and perilous commute over the mountains on Hwy 17. By 1998 I was feeling well situated but stressed due to working long hours hustling signs to cover my growing family and burgeoning overhead.

By then we had moved from our one bedroom house in Felton to a beautiful three bedroom house a few miles away in Ben

Lomond. It was my favorite house because it was yellow and so bright and cheery. I had a nice office with a big window and a little workshop surrounded by two acres of woods. It was a happy time, augmented by the birth of my daughter Jennifer. We lived in a beautiful farmhouse and had lovely antique furniture and many comforts. Our children had lots of fun playing in the big garden and fields and apart from the stress of operating my own business, I was quite content there.

At this time I was also very involved in the *Vaishnava* Hindu community in which my wife and I had met many years before in San Jose. By this time a new rural ashram had been established on thirty beautiful acres in Soquel just twenty minutes away. We often went there during the week for lunch or to participate in special holiday functions as well as the regular Sunday gathering. I had been very active in outreach programs, collection activities and teaching classes. The ashram was the vibrant heart of our community.

HIGH ON A MOUNTAIN

Our house was just adjacent to a public wildlife sanctuary called Quail Hollow that had wonderful sandy trails that wound around a magical mountain with sandstone outcroppings and scrub forest. I drew a great deal of inspiration and stress relief by wandering those trails and releasing my mind and emotions to the wholesomeness of nature. It was my own private meditation spot, because although I was very happy living there, I longed for a simpler and more stress free life and these weekly walks in the woods refreshed and nourished my soul in a special creative way. I wrote many poems about my experiences on that mountain and many insights and realizations about the nature of life and existence came to me in those wholesome natural hours.

Immersing ourselves in nature is probably the best way to heal emotional stress because the forest, seaside and lush grotto offer a unique and primal sanctuary from the mad pace of modern life. These sacred environments are predominated by nature's own vibrational goodness, the quality of *sattva-guna*, natural wholesomeness, and if we open ourselves up to that simple goodness it can easily return our minds to purity and ease.

Often I would engage in a type of walking meditation where I would let go of all intentional thinking processes and energetically empty my self as I walked slowly and aimlessly through the forest allowing my *chi* to flow smoothly and evenly through my body. As I walked I would become increasingly more relaxed and intuitive and begin to *feel the forest*. Amazingly, sometimes I believed the plants and trees were subtly communicating their goodness to me as I walked on, absorbing the energetic goodness and living *chi* around me. There were several times when I even felt the psychic energy of a Native American presence. Like the times when I found stone tools in the creek or an obsidian arrowhead and later had a dream that these were actually revealed to me. Receptivity is a type of psychic sensitivity that can be quite inspiring and personally enriching.

While I was walking in the lovely hills surrounding Quail Hollow and feeling inspired by the commanding view of the surrounding countryside that looks south down the San Lorenzo Valley towards the ocean just barely visible in the distance, I came upon a solitary bench on one of the intermediate promontories that is most agreeable for basking in the sun and gazing at the wide open sky. Below lies a sandy path that winds around the mountain overlooking the wooded valley below. This particular path is so pleasant you can almost feel a sense of goodness emanating from the place. Perhaps it's the feel of this sunny slope or the light color of the sandy path and soft rocks that lends it so much auspiciousness.

As I was wandering there one evening to refresh my spirits from the day's work, I began to tangibly feel the ancient presence of consciousness in the mountain. I came to realize that the whole area had a type of collective consciousness that resembled a whole living organism. The groves of trees and the fields of blossoming flowers, the stream and even the clouds rolling by above my head, demonstrated a unity in diversity that was profoundly united yet dynamically diverse. I felt honored and grateful to feel this abundant energy and the experience increased my appreciation for my awareness of the interconnection with all life on this mountain, on this continent, and on this amazing earth.

Once upon this mountain while playing with the children we carved faces into the soft sandstones with pine twigs. It was a magical family experience. We felt delighted and refreshed as we returned home that evening with laughter and an increased appreciation of this holy hill above our house. As we made our way home I commemorated the experience in a poem that ran thus:

This evening carved a sandstone I,
along the path I found,
removing sandy layers soft,
an ancient face unbound.

Peering out- across the time,
a silent message gave,
to me a wonder,
I thought this —
there's life beyond the grave.

The spirits old of misty past,
yet abide in this great hill,
for heart and thought,
will yet endure,
more than flesh and blood 'ere will.

The secret this,
as yet unknown,
the earth and moon and sun,
they felt this all within themselves,
and knew it all as one.

That time of my life was rich with family, community and growing insight. Although there were many challenges, I was able to relax in nature and nurture my receptivity, which helped me to realize the abundant interconnectedness of all things and this in turn prepared my faith for what was about to come in the spring of 1998.

THE BIG MOVE

My wife Sue is from England and we would visit her parents in Northwood, just north of London, occasionally with the children. That spring we flew over to England with the children and had a very special visit. We were there for almost three weeks and it was as usual, an inspiring and fun filled trip of travel, adventure and family visits. We had several special friends in England at that time that we had met in our travels to India and it was an added treat to spend time with these spiritual family members as well.

We visited the tower of London, the National Galleries at Trafalgar Square and the British Museum with its vast array of artifacts and antiquities spanning many centuries from all over the world.

We love to travel and this trip was especially fun but when we returned home we quickly realized that the party was over. Our landlords had notified us that they were selling the property and that if we liked we could make an offer on the house or we would have to move.

Our landlords at the time were a lovely Asian couple who were so kind and thoughtful. They liked us from the start and although when we first came to enquire about the house there was a crowd of twenty people, all trying to out-bid one another, they took an immediate liking to us, because, as they later explained, *"They liked our energy"*.

Asians generally know about subtle energies and *Feng Shui*. It's part of their culture to energetically read people and places, and when it comes to houses they often know that houses are spaces that hold energies. Because of this, they later explained to us, that they were committed to finding people with "good energy" to live in their house. They knew that residual energies have an effect on the properties, and secondarily, the owners as well. The energies you associate with, will affect your energies, your life and your experience.

We had made it clear that we were spiritually minded vegetarian, non-violent and thoughtful people. That sealed the deal, and although other bidders on the property had offered more money for the place, they gave it to us because they liked us. My daughter had been born in that house and we had spent several happy years there enjoying the children and developing the gardens. But now that beautiful dream was coming to an end and I had to make some hard choices. By then the housing market in the Santa Cruz area had become over-burdened by an influx of dot-com yuppies from Silicon Valley just over the hill.

The once relaxed atmosphere of Santa Cruz had become busier and more congested and rents and property values had gone through the roof. This house in Ben Lomond had cost me $1350.00 in rent every month but now to my dismay as I searched for another property, I realized that I had been getting a really good deal.

Smaller houses with much less room and charm were now renting for $2000 and up. My stress was rising as I realized that not only were all the surrounding properties more expensive, but now they also had droves of people lining up trying to out bid each other!

We were at a disadvantage because no one wanted to rent to a family with children when they could rent to single people or couples with no children, for more money. So there we were, between having to move, and unable to find adequate and affordable accommodation. At this point I realized that there was only one thing to do, and that was surrender to a higher power. You know, once I consciously let go of the self-generated stress of the situation and began to almost mystically relax into the unfolding events, I felt a great relief that opened the abundant energetic flow of new opportunities that followed.

As I mentioned earlier I had been involved with our spiritual community for over 10 years by this time, and naturally when all other options were exhausted, I turned to the thirty acre Ashram property for shelter. Because I was a contributing member of the community in good standing, my request to move onto the Ashram land was almost unanimously approved and soon we began preparations to scale down to the essentials, eliminate the massive amounts of unnecessary objects we had accumulated and begin one of the most powerful and dynamic periods of our lives.

On the outset it looked like a washout. Like everything I had built up to this time was being swept away. But in reality, I was about to be given many powerful and transformative experiences that would create a profound shift in my life, my family and my views of faith, abundance, and what really is truly valuable in life. I was stripped down. Lean and clean and ready to grow.

It was the Greek philosopher Heraclitus of Ephesus who stated thousands of years ago that *"There is nothing permanent but change."* Heraclitus also said: *"You cannot step twice into the same river."* You see, he had realized that abundant change is the natural state of reality, and that reality is endlessly mutable and is flowing like a river in a cyclical procession of movement, like water.

Water is lifted by the sun into the sky as clouds, clouds circle the planet dropping water upon the earth, flowing down the mountains in streams, eventually returning to the ocean of its source. It's the perfect example of the cyclical procession of energetic flow.

In the introduction I mentioned that abundance is not my ability to acquire and guard anything *from* change, but rather, my realization that true abundance is linked to my inner harmony *with* change. Through the power of letting go, the changes I faced became a blessing instead of a burden.

Armed with the optimism that change does not represent loss, but transformation, and transformation is flow and opportunity, we went from living in a beautiful three-bedroom house in the woods with gardens and acreage to a four-man tent pitched on a hillside in Soquel. It was a humbling yet profoundly empowering experience, because I realized that happiness was not produced by what I owned, or acquired, but what I generated and carried within myself. I wrote a poem that expressed my feeling for this shift in perception. I posted it on my refrigerator as we were moving out.

> *Must I own a cup before I can drink?*
> *Shall I buy a chair before I sit?*
> *Do beds and pillows alone define our sleep?*
> *The contents of my heart shall sustain me.*
> *Affection and service is my wealth.*
> *I shall endure these fast coming changes*
> *by dropping attachments one by one*
> *our lightness, brightness, and freedom is won.*

To quote another, more famous poet,
"When ya got nothing,' ya got nothing to lose."

The funny thing is, once I let go of everything I realized everything was an opportunity, and an adventure. I realized the real value resided in my own heart and consciousness. The value and wealth of flexibility. Besides, I had all that I really needed. My family was loving and supportive. I was healthy and optimistic, even philosophically so. My children were happy playing in the woods with the other children of the Ashram, and I was surrounded by an amazing community of friends and spiritual seekers. This was a powerful turning point that brought more abundant flow into my life than I had ever experienced up to that point. Fortunately, I was able to re-frame our experiences into a positive and powerfully transformative change for the whole family that brought about a greater sense of absolute abundance for all of us. As well as a great deal of fun and adventure! Apprehension turned to gratitude and exhilaration. Life became one long epiphany, and I never felt better! Amazingly, my income also shot up and within a year of when I left that hillside to travel the world, I had over $70,000.

MYTHIC STONES

Receptivity opens us up to a great deal of creativity and range of experience that can be quite profound at times.

Once as we were walking along the creek bed in a deep redwood forest, the children and I were examining the many pebbles and stones that lined the sunlit shore. As I looked upon the dappled array, one stone immediately caught my eye. It was an oblong quartz shaft with angled edges. As soon as I picked it up I felt its utility. Its unmistakable potentiality for action in the service of survival.

As I turned the stone in my hand its rough-hewn form with

precise edges suggested a sophisticated and intentionally fashioned ergonomic function. I imagined an individual who may have wandered these forests many thousands of years ago. Some time before this incident I had read an article about the history of the San Lorenzo Valley. The author had mentioned that there had been Native Americans present in this area for nearly 10,000 years. I began to muse over the possibility that this was indeed a stone tool of great antiquity. I had the subtle impression that my experience of the stone was consciously connecting with the residual conscious impressions of the individual, facilitated through the medium of this stone fashioned perhaps a millennium ago. I imagined how the stone could be a link across the vast expanse of time as I began to *"feel"* the stone, not just with my external senses of sight and touch, but also with the deeper comprehension of visionary consciousness. With those impressions I composed this poem in my mind:

> *Delightful stone tool by the stream,*
> *amid the forest my hand it knew,*
> *a face of a thousand summers past,*
> *looking back to me through nature's eye,*
> *where past, present and future unite,*
> *in the ancient timelessness of the inner moment*
> *wise and silent, dark and strong,*
> *the author smiled through my hand,*
> *giving thanks I did in many ways,*
> *for memories of ancient times,*
> *stone weight, gave depth of eye,*
> *and there did touch my heart.*

Since my childhood I've been fascinated by the infinite colors, patterns and variety of shapes to be found in stones. As a child, fossils, rocks, stones, arrowheads, bones and crystals all held a fascination for me and I collected them all in abundance. The beauty and depth of life is all around us, and within us, for everything is an expression of the beauty of the underlying conscious spirit. From microcosm to macrocosm there are infinite layers of subtle and gross manifestations, all emanating from the primal sound vibration, vibrating at various rates to produce the infinite variations of color, form and expression.

The apparently gross physical world that we perceive through our five senses is primarily composed of earth, water, fire, air and ether. These five emerge from consciousness and proceed in a processional manifestation from subtle to gross. In the Vedas, the Bible and the Koran it is represented that in the beginning was the *Word,* or in other words, sound vibration, or rather, energetic vibration. Perhaps from the divine super-subjective consciousness there emerges a primal sound or subtle vibration. This idea of primal sound is represented as AUM in the Vedas. From this subtle primal vibration may arise the ethereal element, then air, then fire and water and earth. From subtle to gross, all these manifestations are perhaps transformations of sound and are themselves sound and motion vibrating at varying rates.

Physicists have found that on the subtle-most level, matter seems to behave as both particle and wave, and that on the sub-atomic level matter has more space between particles than actual particulate mass. In other words, what we see as solid matter is an illusion of actualized thought or consciousness appearing as light and sound. These five elements are perceived, as Aldous Huxley has said; *"through the doors of perception,"* or the five knowledge-acquiring senses of touch, taste, sight, sound, and smell and acted upon by the five working senses such as the tongue, hands, legs, etc. The perceptions of the elements in their various forms are received through the senses into the mind and deliberated upon by the intelligence, which is the feature of mental discernment. All these processes are made manifest and active by the subtlest element of the *jiv-atma* or non-material self, which illuminates and energizes all these secondary elements with conscious light or awareness in the same way the full moon illuminates a cloud in the night. From the deep realizations of the Upanishadic sages we can learn that it is the non-material presence of the self within the body that illumines and activates all these elements through consciousness.

In the writings of the Upanishads, which are the realizations of the prehistoric seers of ancient India, comes the knowledge of the transcendental or non-materially quantifiable spirit soul. The self is non-materially quantifiable, precisely because it is quite paradoxically a "unit" of eternal consciousness, a subjective non-material unit so subtle it cannot be measured by the physical instruments. Eyes that are composed of grosser elements such as earth, water and fire, cannot perceive the subtler elements of air, ether and mind.

The self is said to be an atom of spiritual conscious substance. If modern science were to adopt this spiritual paradigm it might dramatically alter what we myopically consider as appropriate circumstances for the presence of life forms. In other words, if the source of life in biological life forms is recognized as a non-material conscious entity, or eternal sentience, capable of thinking feeling and willing, even in a disembodied state, that would establish the possibility that life could exist under any material circumstance.

If the soul is immutable and indestructible as the Upanishads state, then it is quite conceivable that life forms could exist in such harsh environments as the sun. Causing one to ask the hypothetical question..."*Do fiery leaves on burning trees shade the heads of flaming people?*" Interesting notion isn't it? This earth planet is predominated by water. Our bodies are about 70% water. This is a water planet. Perhaps on other planets there are living souls with bodies composed of fire, or pure intelligence or subtle mental energies, and therefore undetectable by our fleshy eyes composed predominantly of earth, water and fire. Perhaps the moon is a secret citadel of invisible spirits, an invisible civilization of mental energies, undetectable by the physically embodied. Unseen by the fleshy eye, those beings and forms may be perceivable only through intuition, meditation, revelation and dreams. I would often consider ideas such as these upon my pleasant walks in the forest or by the river. Nature has a beautiful way of opening our hearts and minds to greater receptivity, creativity and possibility.

Evening walks can be so inspiring. Especially in the company of those you love. Take time to notice nature's intricate beauty and enormous abundance. It's all around us. Even in the heart of a big city, somewhere there is grass, trees and sky. Let natural abundance inspire you. Its source is divine and pregnant with possibility. It will remind you that your life is remarkable.

Walking in nature is one of the best ways to develop receptivity because the natural environment is often more peaceful than our day-to-day environments. The absence of human-busyness allows our physical and emotional energies to calm down, to relax and to flow more smoothly and evenly. We can find our inner balance in nature. We can relax and become calm, and when we are calm, we are naturally more receptive. *When we are more receptive, we are more perceptive.* The more you can see, the more you will be able to realize, act upon and achieve. This is one possible progression of dynamic growth from the matrix of receptivity.

FLEXIBILITY OF ATTITUDE

In order to gain greater receptivity and flexibility there is one obstacle that must be recognized, understood and dissolved. It's a *"hardening of the attitudes"* that constricts the flow of opportunity, energy and information in our lives. As I mentioned previously, many of our attitudes have been adopted unconsciously by the company that we have kept in the past. We have likes and dislikes. Biased views and constricted understandings of what is possible and probable in our lives, largely due to the types of association we had as a child and adolescent. Most people unconsciously surrender to the dictates of these emotional states and their accompanying misunderstandings, and subsequent limitations. It is our beliefs about what is actually possible that govern how far we reach out to life. Receptivity is directly related to our beliefs. But what are beliefs?

BELIEF AS DYNAMIC POWER

Belief should be flexible as well as receptive. Generally we conceive of belief as an attitude that is rigidly held and maintained despite surrounding change. This type of rigidity can work against us, and my experiences have taught me that belief should be flexible, expansive and able to grow with, and support life. Beliefs that constrict us will choke off opportunities and deny us the abundance and freedom that should be our natural state. Belief is a form of perceptual filtering that has great power. If we tell our selves we cannot do something, then we have already disempowered our ability to achieve that object or outcome. If we tell ourselves we can achieve a certain outcome, then we have allowed ourselves the possibility and freedom to do so, as well as put ourselves in a favorable energetic and emotional state that supports our success. Think about it. If you've lost something, and you tell yourself you'll never find it, you are unnecessarily denying yourself a positive outcome. Remarkably you may even be perceptually occluding your ability to see something that is right in front of you. Something that you would actually recognize if you allowed yourself the belief that it is achievable.

Use belief wisely. Permit yourself the possibility of possibility. Allow yourself at least to choose not to negate what may be possible. Sometimes if we don't know or understand the rules we will go beyond what would have been possible if we believed there were rules or limitations. I remember reading about the Beatles and their amazing songwriting abilities. George Martin, their producer and sound engineer was a classically trained musician. He was amazed by their creative abilities with melody and composition. George Martin recognized that because none of the Beatles could actually read music, they were free of the limitations and constraints that held his creative ability in check. Their ignorance of musical composition turned out to be one of their greatest assets in stretching the boundaries of popular music. Always believe that there is more.

WRESTLING WITH THE TIGER

Our mission as consciously growing and expanding individuals who are reintegrating ourselves into the abundant flow of life is to recognize the hidden agendas, limiting views and unconscious negative states and beliefs within ourselves and overturn them with the light of higher intuitive awareness. A spiritual psychology, if you will. If we measure their value and mercilessly discard these unwanted attitudes, beliefs and societal/cultural biases, (especially if they are not supportive of our health, prosperity and spiritual growth) we will find a new freedom that reinstates us in the abundant consciousness we seek. This is flexibility in action produced by flexible thinking. Allow your beliefs to be alive, allow them to be living and growing states of a flexible conscious awareness.

The mind and imagination have a natural flexibility that becomes apparent at times when the critical factor of the conscious mind is relaxed or disengaged. Imagination, hypnosis, meditation and relaxation are all ways to temporarily suspend this critical factor. While exercising imagination we may notice the critical factor intruding into our new programming space as in the case of a person using affirmations. One may chant positive affirmations over and over again but they may have the opposite result because we can feel the unconscious mind in the form of a small voice or feeling in the background contradicting all that we are affirming. There's something emotionally churning in our gut that undermines the new direction our head is trying to go. We need mental and emotional congruency.

As I mentioned in Chapter One, if we try "not to think" of something we are already captured by that thought, because "trying not" to think of something sets that very "thing" up as the object of our thoughts even though we are telling ourselves we are trying to forget it. If it's a negative idea, the very act of trying to counteract it, is in effect reinforcing it in the unconscious mind, for whatever you fight, you more deeply entangle yourself with. If you wrestle with a problem you will also absorb that problem more deeply into your system. I call this *wrestling with the tiger*. Detachment and observation can powerfully aid you in managing and releasing these states from consciousness. *Insight is higher than action, and action directed by insight becomes skillful action.*

The way to release ourselves from the labyrinth of confusion is to clearly and definitely focus on what we *do* want, because this will effectively nourish the thought pattern we actually desire rather than employing the process of trying to combat (and thereby unconsciously empower) that which we actually wish to release. This is an idea worthy of deep meditation.

HOW I QUIT SMOKING

When I was in my twenties I had been smoking cigarettes for several years and had come to realize that smoking is a self-destructive, unhealthy and expensive addiction. Once I clearly realized this truth I began making plans for my escape from this damaging relationship with tobacco. I tried all of the usual methods like chewing gum, eating more, and bolstering my will power by counting the days I had been without cigarettes. Anyone who's tried to quit smoking knows what this is like.

I would carry on like this for weeks and months always consciously remaining aware of how long I had been *"without"* the thing I was habituated to do but knew was hurting me. These types of inner contradictions can really make our lives miserable. Several times I even made it past the one-year mark only to succumb again to the temptation.

At the time I was working in an office building and several of my fellow employees were also attempting to quit smoking. I noticed that their inability to do so was largely due to the fact that they were constantly reminding themselves of the fact that they were *"trying"* to quit smoking. However, when you *"try"* to do something you are unconsciously telling yourself that you won't be able to do it because you are setting up failure as the dominant background paradigm that you are *"trying"* to work against.

I was finally released from this miserable repetitive pattern by observing the behavior of myself and my contemporaries. I came to the understanding that it was my counting of the days and weeks that kept my mind joined to the idea of smoking and that flexibility of attitude and approach in finding a solution was a key factor in resolving my inner conflict. In effect I gained a deeper insight, which led to more skillful inner representations and actions.

Imagination is far more powerful that willpower. You see, all the while I was feeding my subconscious mind the thought that cigarettes were the actual goal of my behavior. I was inadvertently focusing on what I didn't want (cigarettes) instead of focusing on what I really did want (a life free of even the thought of cigarettes).

Realizing this, I was soon able to consciously release and disentangle myself from the process of counting the days, which in effect, kept me joined to the idea of smoking. From then on I just focused my awareness directly on more constructive matters, ideas and pursuits, and within a short time I had created another thought pattern that became the dominant flow in my consciousness and which completely bypassed the old pattern of thinking. In effect, I rose above the old pattern by the constructive use of imagination.

Rather than wrestling with the issue of smoking or non-smoking, I completely transcended the whole pattern by involving my thought processes in a whole new set of ideas that gave me enthusiasm and energy and excitement about the newer fresher more expansive and abundant life I was consciously creating for myself. Mantra meditation can be particularly useful in this regard. Constantly repeating a phrase, prayer, affirmation or idea bypasses old patterns of thought and releases attention from its previous obsession.

When you congruently and emotionally commit to a course of action you set up success as the dominant background paradigm and invariably you set in motion the personal power and imagination which all work together to bring about more consistent and dramatic results. Strong desire coupled with imagination and flexibility is virtually unstoppable.

Once I clearly saw the limiting and destructive nature of cigarette smoking, it set in motion the cognitive energies that led to release from the addictive pattern of thinking. Flexibility of approach enabled a more elegant solution. Higher perspective and better association sealed the deal.

Imagination is power. Flexibility is its nature.

RECEPTIVITY OF THE BODY

With clarity of purpose, receptivity and flexibility of attitude we are now ready to work on the body. The body reflects the mind and the predominant paradigm held consistently in the mind will produce noticeable changes in the body. Our physiological and psychological states move in a dynamic loop, continually affecting one another.

If you feel depressed you can often lift your spirits by changing your physiology, like going for a walk or a run. Also doing yoga or hiking in nature will quickly change your physiology and thus alter your psychological state for the better. Movement affects mentality. Exercise is a proven mood enhancer. It releases endorphins in the brain, it activates all systems, and it moves, circulates and invigorates the whole organism. Healthy bodies are moving bodies. Regular exercise is one of the most important gifts you can give yourself. It is transformative. It is life affirming.

I like to put on my favorite music and dance to it in the morning. It doesn't take but a few songs to significantly raise your heart rate. Walking, running, hiking are all good but dancing is the king of exercise because it also significantly enhances and uplifts your mood. It's hard to dance wildly and remain depressed or sad, especially when the music is passionate. If you dance to kirtan, your exercise can also be a meditation, uplifting your heart, mind and body.

Conditioning the body towards greater receptivity and abundance begins with harmonizing our health with the energetic patterns of nature's flow. When we utilize the understanding of *Unity in Diversity* we gain a great advantage that goes beyond "balance" which is basically a fictitious state of equilibrium. Undynamic "balance" can lead to a lack of vitality or a feeling of being stuck. *Unity in Diversity* teaches us that everything is moving, and that when there is harmony amongst the diverse energies there is a kind of dynamic equilibrium that is healthy. Our personal energetic patterns and psychology as well as the environment are always on the go. Energy that is static is dead or dying. Our task of harmonizing with the abundant flow of life is to bring our energies into a dynamic and living adjustment with the seasonal, planetary and universal principles that govern life and the energetic flow of all energies.

THE SCIENCE OF LIFE

Through my many travels in India and Asia I learned of Ayurveda, which is India's 5,000 year old science of life. More than just an indigenous herbal medical system, it's the art of living in harmony with nature, and it explains the nature of everything in the universe in terms of energetic patterns. When we learn about Ayurvedic principles, we learn about ourselves, how our energy flows in relation to the environment and the seasons. We also learn how we can be our healthiest and happiest at all times by harmonizing our own energetic patterns with the particular time, place and circumstances of our surroundings. Harmony is an ongoing dynamic process, and requires our attention and observation.

The Ayurvedic healing system of India is a traditional holistic medical system many thousands of years old that views the body according to three humors. In the Sanskrit language they are called *doshas*. Here's a brief explanation of these three doshas or energetic models.

VATA AIR TYPE

Vata-type people are generally thin and find it hard to gain weight. Because of this, *vatas* have very little energy reserve and can tire easily and allow themselves to fall out of harmony. *Vatas* need to get sufficient rest and not overdo things, stay warm, and keep a regular lifestyle routine. The *vata* dosha controls all movement in the body, including breathing, digestion, and nerve impulses from the brain. When *vata* is out of harmony, anxiety and other nervous disorders may be present. Digestive problems, constipation, cramps, and even premenstrual pain usually are attributed to a *vata* imbalance. The most important thing to know about *vata* is that it leads the other *doshas. Vata* usually goes out of balance first, which causes the early stages of disease. More than half of all illnesses are *vata* disorders. Balancing *vata* is important for everyone, because when *vata* is in balance, the other two doshas, *pitta* and *kapha* are generally in harmony as well.

PITTA FIRE TYPE

Pitta-type people are generally of medium size and well proportioned. They have a medium amount of physical energy and stamina. They also tend to be intelligent and have a sharp wit and a good ability to concentrate. Fire is a characteristic of *pitta,* whether it shows up as fiery red hair or a short temper. Since *pittas'* body temperature is generally warm, *pitta* types can go out of balance with overexposure to the sun. Their eyes are often sensitive to light. They are ambitious by nature and also can be very demanding and abrasive. *Pitta* types are known for their strong digestion but should be careful not to abuse it. Their heat makes them particularly thirsty, and they should take caution not to douse their *agni,* or digestive fire, with too much liquid during meals. *Pitta dosha* leads us to crave moderation and purity. We rely on *pitta* to regulate our intake of food, water, and air. Any toxins, such as alcohol or tobacco, show up as a *pitta* imbalance in the body. Toxic emotions such as jealousy, intolerance, and hatred also should be avoided to keep *pitta* in balance for optimum health.

KAPHA WATER TYPE

Kapha-type people tend to have sturdy, heavy frames, providing a good reserve of physical strength and stamina. This strength gives *kaphas* a natural resistance to disease and a generally positive outlook about life. The *kapha dosha* is slow, and *kapha* types tend to be slow eaters with slow digestion. They also may tend to speak slowly. They are calm and affectionate but, when out of balance, can become stubborn and lazy. They learn slowly, with a methodical approach, but also retain information well with a good understanding of it. *Kapha dosha* controls the moist tissues of the body, so a *kapha* imbalance may show up as a cold, allergies, or asthma. These imbalances may become aggravated in the cold, wet winter months. Cold and wet weather aggravates *kapha,* and therefore warmer climates may be helpful. They should not dwell in the past or resist change. They need lots of exercise and need to be careful not to overeat. *Kaphas* need stimulation to bring out their vitality. *Kapha dosha* teaches us steadiness and a sense of well being.

THE AYURVEDIC CLASSIFICATION OF FOOD

The food we eat is not just food for the body but also food for the mind. According to Ayurveda there are three categories.

1. *Sattvic* or sentient: Food that is good for the body and mind, e.g. fresh vegetables, fruits, nuts, milk products and grains. These foods are natural, wholesome and organic.

2. *Rajasic* or energetic: These foods are good for the body but are unsettling for the mind and tend to be energizing. They are hot and spicy like chilies, coffee, alcohol, curry, etc. Foods of this type are typically hot, spicy and energizing.

3. *Tamasic* or static: This food may or may not be good for the body but is definitely darkening to the mind e.g. meat, fish, eggs, preserved foods, mushrooms, and intoxicants and habituating drugs of all kinds. Foods of this type are processed, old, decaying, and lacking vitality.

With the clarity that comes from understanding the Ayurvedic energetic body types and food groups, you will begin to learn how to dynamically adjust your bodily energies to time place and circumstance. This brings an incredible advantage and flexibility of approach. The body types of *vata, pitta* and *kapha* are themselves not fixed or static patterns but are also continually moving within our systems. We may have a dominant body type such as *Pitta,* which will color the energies of our biological and psychological processes but we need to be aware that all three of the *doshas* are continually competing for supremacy in our system at any given time and that they may change daily, monthly and seasonally. Once you become acquainted with their nature and symptoms and are able to identify the *doshic* patterns in your own physiology you will be able to grow into a profound understanding of their subtle operations in yourself and the environment.

THE FIVE SHEATHS

In addition to these three *doshas* or energy types, Ayurveda describes five layers of material energy called *sheaths* that are densities of matter covering our individual consciousness. These are the five sheaths.

The food sheath is composed of the physical form that is produced by the foodstuffs we consume. These foods are made up of the three energetic modalities of *sattva, rajas* and *tamas,* or illumination, activity and obscurity. *Sattvic* foods are important as they promote higher awareness and better health than *rajarshic* or *tamasic* foods.

The breath sheath mediates between the physical and emotional bodies. If the mind and emotions are disturbed, they can be calmed through regulated breathing.

The emotional sheath is our inner world of subjective feeling where emotional states take turns rising and falling like love, affection, compassion, lust and attraction, anger, greed, generosity, happiness and sorrow. These emotions color our consciousness according to the predominance of the modes, of *sattva, rajas and tamas.*

The intelligence sheath is the feature of the mind that discerns between one thought and another, one quality and another. In the worldly sense this is our *buddhi* or intelligence that helps us discriminate between qualities and dualities. In the higher sense it is our *dharma-buddhi* or spiritual intelligence that awakens us to the pursuit of our inner growth and comprehensive understanding.

The bliss sheath is the causal body that is centered in the heart and is the abode of our innermost vitality called *ojas* as well as our *pranic* life force. It is related to the subtle ground of creation and is related to the field of unlimited potentiality. It is accessed in deep sleep and profound meditation.

Dr. David Frawley has written a highly acclaimed book on this subject titled *Ayurvedic Healing.* I encourage you to explore this fascinating subject of Ayurveda, *"the science of life."*

FOOD AND THE MIND

As I mentioned in chapter one, the mind is one aspect of the subtle body, or aura of the conscious self, which receives the impressions of the senses. The brain is its physical organ. However, Ayurvedic psychology considers the mind as a focused point of sentience. Along with the intelligence and ego it functions on the subtle level behind and through the physical organism of the brain.

Nature works through the mind, which is the source of its varied structures and operations. It is the fundamental ground of objective material manifestation and is the basic constituent of *prakriti* (matter). In Ayurveda, the mind is considered a subtle material element and is colored by the energetic modalities of the foods we eat. If we eat a predominantly *tamasic* (decaying, lacking fresh vitality) diet our mental tendencies will move towards ignorance, depression and opacity. If we eat a predominantly *sattvic* (fresh, healthy & clean) diet our minds will gain greater clarity and uplifting illumination. *Rajarshic* foods (filled with energy, fire and heat) will cause our minds to be lusty, ambitious, unsteady and distracted. We build the qualitative energy of the mind by the quality of the foods we eat. The nature of the mind is also colored by the sense impressions we absorb in our daily life from our interactions with others, the types of films we watch regularly, the music we listen to, and actions we habitually perform in our daily lives.

THE FOUR LEVELS OF THE MIND

Chitta – The *chitta* is the general field of mental experience, which includes the unconscious. The *chitta* is related to the air element and its underlying quality is the *tamasic* qualities of ignorance and fear. The animal kingdom is predominated by this level of mind because the higher discriminating factor of *buddhi* or intelligence is lacking, animals are involved in the fight or flight level of existence and are unable to rationalize or mentally rise above their circumstances. In the wild, fear predominates in the mental experience of animals as a survival mechanism.

Manas – *Manas* is the portion of the mind that interacts with the senses and includes the emotional arena of feeling and sensation and is related to the water element. This level of mind is predominated by desire and is the predominant arena for the human activities of desire and acquisition, happiness and distress, loss and gain. It is *rajarshic* or passionate in nature and its nature is therefore distracted, attached, bewildered and ultimately productive of sorrow.

Ahankar – The *ahankar* is the self-conscious ego of differentiated identity. It creates the sense of separateness from other beings and gives rise to pride, arrogance, anger and aggression. It is related to the earth element and obscures the higher intuitive insight of *buddhi* or intelligence. Because it is *asuric* and *tamasic* in nature it gives rise to an aggressive expansion of the exploitive and dominating mood towards objective nature or *prakriti*. Humanity is currently plagued by this level of the exploitive mind. We are experiencing the pernicious effects in the form of social and national conflict as well as environmental destruction. These are all products of the exploitive dualistic mind colored by *ahankar*.

Buddhi – This is the higher feature of discriminating intelligence. It is related to fire and illumination and has a *sattvic* or uplifting quality, although it can be adversely affected by *rajas* (passion) and *tamas* (ignorance). In its purity, *buddhi* is an instrument of direct perception and intuitive inner growth. It can function in a lower as well as higher way. Its lower expression is merely caught up in the identification with worldly concerns.

When functioning in a higher spiritual expression it becomes *dharma-buddhi* or that pure *sattvic (suddha-sattvic)* expression of the soul that leads the conscious individual self out of the delusion of misidentification with matter. In effect, assisting the liberation of consciousness to its full abundant spiritual expression.

Buddhic application of intelligence is a foundational key to Ayurvedic healing because Ayurveda aims to turn the materially directed *buddhi* towards a higher understanding of consciousness as the basis of reality, which is the wholesale cure for all mental and physical distress and disease. It is the gateway to the unlimited abundance of consciousness, the absolute abundance of the soul.

Because the mind has a very subtle and mobile nature it is as difficult as the wind to control. It has an almost autonomous and dualistic nature that impresses its expression of the three energetic modalities upon our awareness in the forms of *sattva, rajas* and *tamas.* We become caught up in the confusion and identification with these modes and thereby are bewildered in our attempts to understand and control the mind. *Sattvic* intelligence or *buddhi,* aids awareness in separating itself from the muddled confusion of this misidentification.

When the intelligence is outwardly directed it is caught up in the identification with worldly concerns, which gives rise to a materialistic paradigm of life wherein the pursuit of pleasure and materialistic expansion through the conquest of nature are paramount. Science may aid this misuse of intelligence when its development follows the progression of exploration, exploitation, domination and militarization.

When functioning in a higher spiritual expression, *buddhi* becomes the search for truth, clarity and the wisdom that leads the individual out of the delusion of misidentification with matter by assisting the liberation of consciousness to its full spiritual expression.

Ignorance is the *tamasic* quality of mistaking one thing for another. It is a lack of pure and clear perception of reality. It is a mistaken view of ourselves and the environment. The mind arises from a basic state of *tamas* or ignorance and therefore the mind cannot rise above itself. Only the higher intuition of pure *sattvic* intelligence can transcend the materially conditioned mind.

One of the most important things you can learn in life is how to use your mind and thinking processes in the most efficient and beneficial way. Mind states or mental concepts are perceptual filters, which I briefly mentioned in Chapter One. Perceptual filtering is how I represent experience to myself, in my own mind, and the values I apply to experiences. Many of these mind states are unconscious processes. Some people go through their whole life and miss this most important key to success and happiness.

THE MIND AND SUBTLE SENSES

Most of us are familiar with the Western psychological concept of the gradations of mind. Over the last century these ideas have grown from the field of motivational psychology. In the 1950's Dr. Maxwell Matlz, Vernon Howard and many others pioneered these ideas. Prior to them, Sigmund Freud and Carl Gustav Jung explored and developed the modern foundations of psychology. Today most of us take it for granted that we all have a higher or super-conscious mind, a conscious or everyday waking mind and an unconscious or subconscious mind.

The Ayurvedic view is that the radiance of the non-material conscious self gives rise to the higher intuitive mind. In Ayurvedic life science this radiance of the self contains the five *tanmatras* or subtle idea forms of the inner sense organs, corresponding to the outer sense organs of eyes, ears, mouth, skin and nose and their corresponding objects. In dreams we experience these *tanmatras,* which are likened to subtle archetypal blueprints of the working and knowledge-acquiring senses we use in our daily experience, such as the eyes, ears, nose, etc. The senses themselves are perceptual channels by which we apprehend objective experience as well as project our subjective states. ESP or psychic experiences of clairvoyance are produced by the actions of these inner subtle senses and can be experiences of the higher or intuitive mind.

Carl Jung has dealt extensively with the nature of the unconscious or subconscious mind, which is the repository of all of our sensory experiences as well as the collective unconscious aggregate of all humanity's experiences. In the East this is related with the *akash* or subtle vibratory record of the etheric nature that contains traces of the thoughts, words and deeds of all of humanity, throughout time.

From the subtle self arises the penumbra of self, called mind, and the intelligence or *buddhi,* which is the discerning factor of the mind. The mind is the subtle repository of the impressions received through the senses. Emotions arise as our inner response to these impressions. Understanding the relationships between these perceptual factors awakens the wisdom born of insight and experience. It is a great meditative science known as the *samkhya* (counting) philosophy in India.

Most of us in the West consider that the mind is basically composed of two levels: The conscious mind and the unconscious or subconscious mind.

A third level of super-consciousness becomes active when the inner brightness of the self is more clearly revealed, especially due to inner purification through yoga practice. At this point a higher intuitive mind begins to manifest the deeper wisdom inherent in the spiritual self. Psychic experiences such as ESP, clairaudience and clairvoyance are symptoms of this type of awakening, which are rare but sometimes are awakened in highly developed persons and advanced practitioners of meditation and yoga.

MYSTIC ABUNDANCE

Rare persons who reach a high level of mental and yogic self-mastery may begin to manifest psychic powers. These mystic powers are well known to the followers of *kundalini-yoga,* which is the eightfold path of self-mastery outlined by the sage Patanjali in his *yoga-sutras.*

Patanjali's eightfold path of yoga aims the aspirant at the final goal of super-conscious Samadhi, which is a state of exclusive absorption in divine consciousness. This Samadhi is not an impersonal union of the soul with the divine, but a unified communion that maintains the absolute unity yet paradoxical diversity of the individual soul and the supreme soul. It is a union in diversity that ultimately leads to the exchange of ecstatic divine emotions called *rasa,* in the playful enlightened stages of *lila,* or ecstatic divine pastimes.

EIGHTFOLD PATH OF YOGA

Patanjali's eightfold path of yoga consists of the following eight practices.

Yama – a code of high conduct and self-restraint, such as celibacy and righteous conduct.

Niyama – religious observances, vows and commitments to practice, such as study and devotion.

Asana – integration of mind and body through physical activity such as selfless service and the mastery of the physical body by means of *hatha yoga* postures.

Pranayama – regulation of breath leading to integration of mind and body producing mental focus.
Pratyahara – withdrawal of the senses of perception from their objects, leading to inner unity.

Dharana – concentration, one-pointedness of mind leading to deeper states of mental clarity and focus.

Dhyana – deepening meditation that leads to the attainment of Samadhi, union with the Divine.

Samadhi – the profound experience of blissful divine awareness in the super-conscious state wherein the yogi constantly sees the *param-atma* or supreme soul within his own heart and soul.

When the mind has been trained to remain fixed on a certain internal or external location there comes to it the power of flowing in an unbroken current towards that point. This state is called *dhyana*. When one has so intensified the power of *dhyana* as to be able to reject the external part of perception and remain meditating only on the internal part, that state is called *samadhi*.

When the imprisoned splendor of the soul is released and realized there are no more karmic traces to be suffered or enjoyed as the soul abandons its illusory misidentification with material form and consciousness is released into its unlimited potential. This is the absolute abundance of conscious existence and bliss. *Sat-chit-ananda*.

Even before *samadhi*, at the threshold of *dhyana* there is the awakening of mystic powers, called *siddhis* or perfections in yogic terminology. These are miraculous psychic powers that appear with deepening states of concentration at the dawning of super-consciousness. The yoga schools consider them a distraction from the actual goal of *samadhi* and they are rarely pursued as a goal in themselves. The *bhakti-yoga* school of the Gaudiya lineage, view *siddhis* as by-products of the higher spiritual conduct of service and *kirtan* and many saints are known to have attained them as by-products of their deep devotional lifestyle. Several of the miracles performed by Christ can be understood to be the demonstration of these yogic perfections.

SIDDHIS - YOGA PERFECTIONS

The *Bhagavata Purana* describes the eight yoga *siddhis*:

Anima: reducing one's body even to the size of an atom.

Mahima: expanding one's body to an infinitely large size.

Garima: becoming infinitely heavy.

Laghima: becoming almost weightless.
Prapti: having unrestricted access to all places.
Prakamya: realizing whatever one desires.
Isṭva: possessing absolute lordship.
Vastva: the power to subjugate all.

These descriptions of psychic powers may seem fantastic or merely mythological to us who are far removed from the grand traditions of a society steeped in austerity, discipline and heroic self-mastery such as we find in the ancient histories of India. However, these descriptions indicate only a fraction of the immense powers inherent in the mind of man, which are achievable by deep insight and self-mastery in yoga. They indicate that we are using so little of our achievable potential. They demonstrate the fact that our souls and minds have an absolute abundance far greater than what we presently perceive.

THE THREE MODES OF NATURE

Besides the *doshas* or body types, Ayurveda also delineates the three primary modes in nature, which are related to the *doshas,* these are called the *tri-gunas,* or three modes of nature. As I explained previously in relation to the Ayurvedic classification of food, the three modes are:

Illumination *(Satva guna)*
Energy *(Rajo guna)*
Inertia *(Tamo guna)*

Sometimes these modes are described as representing *goodness, passion and ignorance.* Everything is affected by these modes. They are energetic patterns or energy systems that govern environments, food, people, thoughts and activities.

When we awake in the morning and feel groggy — that's the mode of inertia or *tamas.* How do we get out of that modality?

Many people will drink coffee. Coffee is in the mode of *rajas* or energy. Caffeine gives an energy buzz that gets you moving. Exercise will do the same thing for it is also *rajarshic* in nature.

Tamas is characterized as darkness, ignorance, lethargy, and obscuration. Intoxication is a symptom of this mode of ignorance and it often mistakes one thing for another by accepting what is actually damaging as being beneficial, hence it is called the mode of ignorance. Some forms of *tamas* and *rajas* are biologically essential, like sleep and sex respectively. There is no morality attributed to them. They are simply energetic modalities, necessary for balance.

Smoking cigarettes is a good example of *tamas*. Everyone knows it leads to the destruction of the physical organism through cancer, emphysema etc. Yet millions will smoke because *it tastes good*. Inhaling poisonous smoke tastes good? This is the mode of ignorance. The act of *ignor-ing* the reality of its damaging effects.

Meat is decomposing flesh. Consuming it creates disease in the body. Supporting its sale perpetuates slaughterhouses and recycles violence and fear in human society. If the human social body is predominantly violent, destructive and greedy, we need only look at the diet, both food and media-wise, to understand that the *rajarshic and tamasic* modalities are operating.

Television and films are big-time social programmers. Most are *tamasic* and *rajarshic*. A good example of this would be horror films *(tamasic)* and action films *(rajarshic)*. These ideas of the modes can also be applied to music. You can often check the mode you're predominantly in by examining your diet of food, film and music. We are merely describing energetic modes here and how they blend in our lives and color our thoughts and activities as well. Everything we think, do or say is colored by the *tri-gunas*.

What we consume as food also dramatically affects our consciousness and inner energetic systems. Foods that are fresh, clean, natural, organic and free from the subtle taint of killing, are in the mode of goodness or *sattva*...illumination. Such foods will promote health and higher thinking and are good for gaining the clarity necessary for meditation on higher realities. They are the healthiest type of foods.

If those *sattvic* foods are further energized with prayer or grateful intentions they become spiritually potent as well and over time are able to diminish negative karmic stains in the unconscious mind. *Sattvic* foods can be energetically transformed by grateful and sincere prayer. Such eating becomes an act of worship and purification. It becomes a meditation that everything is essentially conscious substance in transformation. The food we eat, the air we breathe and the earth beneath our feet are all transformations of conscious energies. You will find over the course of several months after adopting a *sattvic* lifestyle, the energy patterns in your life will begin to shift, brighten and open up. Negativities of thought and behavior will fall away and be replaced by more conscious loving behavior patterns, such as mindfulness, insight and compassion.

You will notice a remarkable lightness and clarity that will bring about a greater energetic flow of abundance in all areas of your life. I encourage you to study these modes and observe and manage them in your daily life. You will realize a higher level of empowerment by doing so.

THE PREVENTION OF AGING

Another aspect of Ayurveda I'd like to share with you is the prevention of aging called *rasayana* therapy. Aging is an inevitable change for all biological organisms. For most people growing old is not welcome for it exchanges our youthful appearance for what is often perceived as a less attractive state.

We live in a modern culture obsessed by youth and beauty. In traditional cultures, senior citizens are more likely to be appreciated for their wisdom and experience. In cultures that are pious and spiritually oriented, elders are not perceived as being *over the hill* or past their productive years but are ideally persons who have not only gained the worldly wisdom of their years but deep spiritual wisdom and merit as well. Like fine wines, their value increases with age.

The West is gradually gaining greater appreciation for these qualities in older people and larger sections of society are learning to grow old more gracefully and lead more productive lives well into their seventh and eighth decades. My wife's parents lived a balanced life in a regulated manner, which incorporated long daily walks and moderate habits, which in the long run, helped them live long and happy lives. By following the principles of Ayurveda it is not only possible to slow down the process of aging and restore physical and mental strength but also prevent the consequences of aging to a great extent. In Ayurveda old age is called *jara,* and is of two types.

Kalaja jara- timely aging

Akala jara- premature aging

Timely aging means that gradual seasoning that comes naturally to every one. In Ayurveda, the human body has been defined as *"jiryate anena iti shareera"* which means it is decaying and decomposing at every moment. To grow old is inevitable, but to grow old gracefully is a great blessing.

Change and age are inevitable. But the process of aging can be slowed down by following the correct *rasayana* therapy. The onset and manifestation of aging and the characteristics of each succeeding decade can be postponed by using the appropriate *rasayana* therapy. From birth, every individual is bestowed with a specific constitution. According to their unique constitution or *prakruti,* each individual will suffer the corresponding effects of aging. *Vata,* or persons with air dominated constitutions are prone to suffer from dry rough skin, anxiety and weight loss. *Pitta* or firey persons are prone to suffer from premature graying, loss of hair, wrinkles, and skin rashes or infections. Persons with a *Kapha* or watery constitution are prone to suffer from weight gain, depression and congestive conditions.

Akalajara is premature aging or early onset of aging and often comes to those who have unhealthy diets and irregular hours combined with negative behavior traits. The two main categories for its debilitating effects are diet and lifestyle.

DIET

Some dietary causes of *akalajara* are excessive intake of sour, salty and pungent foods or too much intake of red meat, or very light food. Another factor is incompatible, or unsuitable diet according to one's body type or *dosha.* Excessive dry and alkali food, heavy foods, untimely eating, irregular food habits and poor food combinations are all things to avoid.

LIFESTYLE

Some of the lifestyle patterns that increase the onset of *akalajara,* or premature aging, are sleeping in the daytime, staying up late at night, excessive indulgence in sex, excessive indulgence in alcohol and smoking, continual fear or anxiety, anger, depression, lust, or excessive physical exertion. Excesses of all kinds tend to wear us down. Moderation is always beneficial.

These inappropriate diets and irregular behaviors can greatly contribute to premature aging. Following a regulated and balanced sleeping pattern bestows health and longevity, contentment and strength. Staying up late and awakening in the nighttime can cause the *vata* or air element to become vitiated, which induces dryness in the body and disturbance to the mind.

We all know how mental states like fear, anxiety, and depression affect the body and cause many psychosomatic disorders. These are some of the precipitating factors for early aging and are symptoms of an imbalance in the air element.

RASAYANA: YOUTHFUL REJUVENATION

The word *rasayana* contains two words *rasa* and *ayana*. *Rasa* means the body fluid, which is responsible for the nourishment of the entire body. *Ayana* means to direct in a proper way, or to bestow. This *rasa* circulates in the entire body, and penetrates into minute channels and nourishes the body. This *rasa* should be of good quality and should be in adequate quantity. It should also be properly circulated to provide the nourishment the cells need, enabling a healthy and long life. This *rasa* can be compared to lymph and circulates in the body eventually transforming into *dhatus*. If *rasa* is deficient in quality or quantity there will be a deficiency to all the *dhatus* or basic tissues, leading to various diseases.

BENEFITS OF RASAYANA THERAPY

Rasayan rejuvenation therapy can significantly contribute to the promotion of memory, intelligence, and immune strength bolstering us against disease and decay. It also assists in maintaining optimum strength of the body and senses. It increases mental clarity and comprehension as well as the promotion of a glowing complexion. To prevent the effects of premature old age and to attain a healthy and long life, *rasayana* therapy is the best choice. To prevent premature aging, *achara rasayana* is the best *rasayana* therapy.

ACHARA RASAYANA

Achara rasayana is a mode of living that encompasses both behavior and conduct. It is a code of conduct that leads to a stress-free life, which in turn positively effects longevity. We live in a highly stressed society due to the technological acceleration of our lives. These important principles can assist us to live longer lives of greater quality and contentment.

BENEFICIAL CONDUCT

Make it your habit to always speak pleasant and truthful words. Learn to maintain mental peace and emotional composure. Through insight and practice, learn to gain greater control over the mind. You should be optimistic and courageous under all circumstances. Another very beneficial practice is the daily reciting of prayers, hymns, mantras or positive and uplifting literatures. Seek to associate with high-minded people of good conduct. Learn to practice kindness towards all living things, including plants and animals. Develop a sincere, respectful and friendly attitude towards elders, teachers, parents, learned ones and Divinity as you conceive Divinity to be. Piety, healthy habits and thoughts, and philanthropy are also beneficial.

UNBENEFICIAL CONDUCT

Unbeneficial behaviors include anger, violence and jealousy, excessive indulgence in violent films, liquor, drugs and excessive sex. Also fatigue due to excessive strain or over-endeavor, rough speech, cruel and harmful acts are considered unbeneficial. All of these behaviors contribute to stress and unhappiness. They should be avoided as much as possible.

CELIBACY

Celibacy is not something that is highly regarded in our modern society. Its practice tends to be exclusively sequestered in the monastic or deeply religious sections of society. These days it is not uncommon for teenagers to begin their sexual exploration during their formative years, yet according to Ayurveda this has a weakening effect on the organism. The ages from birth to twenty are the most important as the body is building tissue, and in a man the *sukra-dhatu* or semen is the essence of all the *dhatus,* or bodily tissues. In yogic literature the analogy is given that it takes one hundred drops of blood to make one drop of semen or *sukra.* Great vitality and *pranic* life-force potency called *ojas* is housed in the *sukra* and when it is expelled in the sexual act, a great deal of vital energy is lost from the body. This is why in traditional Indian culture the male children were trained in strict celibacy as part of the educational curriculum.

When young people were trained to remain celibate through their teens they developed great intellectual, moral and physical luster as well as inner strength that benefits society as a whole. This system is still current in some places in India today, though much of Asia is now becoming influenced by Western habits and lifestyles. When the *sukra dhatu,* which is the essence of all the *dhatus,* is restored in the body through celibate retention it imparts a great strength to the body and remarkable powers to the mind. Even moderation of sexual activity will be quite beneficial, and in this day and age, moderation is often a more reasonable approach.

TRANSFORMING EXPERIENCE

This morning there were some homeless fellows across the street from my house. They were clearly intoxicated and channeling some dark energies by loudly expressing violence and negativity. They were clearly predominated by *tamo-guna,* the energetic mode of decay and darkness. Often through excessive substance abuse, the inner aura, intelligence and will power weaken and succumb to negative subtle energies. Psychedelics in particular will damage the subtle body, opening it up to subtle parasitic negative influences, but prolonged alcohol abuse can also have a similar effect over time.

Those fellows in the street were in need of love, kindness and compassion. The best course would be to give them spiritually charged foodstuffs in *sattva-guna*, the energetic mode of illumination, clarity and light, for that would energetically purify, uplift and transform them from the inside out without any effort on their part. However, this sort of benefit is slow to manifest and will require repeated *sattvic* diet and association.

The circumstances did not allow for this so, from some distance I began reciting Sanskrit prayers, ringing a bell, offering up incense and throwing holy Ganges water in their direction. They soon quietly left of their own accord with my blessings and prayers for their purification and growth. Over the last 25 years of teaching yoga I've witness countless individuals transform their lives by moving their predominant energetic base from the *tamasic* to the *sattvic* mode.

Typically someone predominated by *tamas* will sleep late, procrastinate, make excuses, blame others, be morose, argumentative, irritable, atheistic, slow moving, take intoxication, eat meat and generally be unclean in thought word and deed. They are typically fond of unclean or unkempt appearances and environments. A *tamasic* lifestyle is like living in the shadows.

Predominantly *rajarshic* people tend to be very quick, firey, passionate, ready to fight or take on a challenge, materially motivated, often multi-tasking, with many projects and ideas, fond of hot spicy foods, alcohol and stimulants. A *rajarshic* lifestyle is always on the go and attracted to busy urban areas, nightclubs and excessive activities.

By contrast, those with a *sattvic* lifestyle will tend to rise early, be attracted to prayer and meditation, be peaceful and have faith in a higher power. They will tend to eat light, clean and beneficial vegetarian foods, be optimistic, be clean in thought word and deed, be helpful, kind and considerate, broad-minded and eager to learn and share. They are often fond of natural lush environments. A *sattvic* lifestyle is predominantly peaceful.

Most people are a combination of all three, and you can witness the modes as they predominate at certain times of the day and night. I worked for years with the public, engaged in fund-raising activities and many times witnessed the effects of these modes upon large groups of people during the various times of day and night.

In the early morning *sattva* will predominate. It's very peaceful at dawn. By mid morning the *rajasic* energy kicks in until about noon. People tend to move more slowly in the afternoons as *tamasic* energy comes into play, but gain a second wind by twilight when *sattva* briefly makes another appearance, followed by another *rajarshic* period, and by 10pm *tamas* begins to set in again heralding sleep. Of course these are generalizations that will also be colored by the types of environments we frequent as well as the movements of the modes throughout our day and night. We can think of it as a color palate with the three modes as our three primary colors and by combining them we get millions of other color combinations in the form of subtle shades of energy, thought and behavior. Some cultural groups have predominant modes as well. Bengalis, the Irish and Latinos, all tend to be passionate, intense, fond of spicy foods and romantic, all *rajo-guna* characteristics.

Observe yourself, your thoughts and behavior. Try to identify the predominant modes as they shift throughout the day. Observe the people and environments that surround you. What energetic modes predominate in them? See how you can balance and adjust energies and people by using these modes and applying your growing understanding of their operations.

It's a powerful type of knowledge that will benefit you in many ways and lead to a more insightful experience of Absolute Abundance.

FASTING AND ABUNDANCE

In the past 40 years people have become more health conscious than ever and many are beginning to appreciate the benefits of fasting. Fasting may be defined as a period of complete abstinence from all types of food or certain specific foods. Contrary to the common perception that fasting is a form of harsh austerity, on closer examination it may turn out to be a beneficial holiday for the body. In our modern lifestyles fasting is a rare phenomenon but is second nature to animals, which instinctively avoid food to ease pain, discomfort or disease.

Often people are wary of fasting, fearing they may damage their health in some way. However, according to A. J. Carlson, Professor of Physiology, University of Chicago, a healthy person can remarkably survive for up to 50-75 days without food. Of course such intense fasting programs should only be undertaken in acute cases of disease with a physicians' guidance, and only in the absence of other health problems or emotional stress. Remarkably, each pound of human fat is equivalent to 3,500 calories, and even one pound of superfluous extra fat is enough to provide the required calories for a full day of strenuous physical exertion. That means that many of us have a great abundance of extra energy stored within our bodies that can be safely burned off through the process of regular fasting and exercise.

My personal experiences with fasting have shown me that I actually have more and better quality energy when I fast. As my system becomes cleaner, the energy within my body flows more smoothly and abundantly. As a result I become more receptive, intuitive and insightful. When you lift the burdens of a clogged biology you bring better quality of receptivity into play.

Most of us are unaware that the body requires abundant energy to digest food. Fasting enables a much-needed rest for the overworked digestive system, and this saved energy goes into self-healing and the repairing of damaged systems. It's a scientifically proven fact that cleansing and detoxification in the intestines, blood and cells heals the body from many ailments. Fasting thus invigorates the immune system and stimulates the whole body to function at its optimum level promoting physical, emotional and mental health. Fasting rejuvenates the entire body, bringing greater clarity of mind, balanced emotional states as well as refined receptivity.

Here are some of the amazing benefits of fasting.

• Finding relief from a variety of health disorders begins by making lifestyle changes. Supervised fasting for a stipulated period assists an individual to make those required changes in their life that will positively influence their health.

• Fasting aids in overcoming addictions to all types of drugs including caffeine, nicotine, marijuana and alcohol. Fasting helps lower withdrawal symptoms, which commonly deter people from overcoming addictions.

• Fasting helps lower cholesterol.

• Fasting aids in eliminating gastrointestinal disorders like constipation, bloating, and gastritis.

• A supervised fasting program can assist diabetics to make crucial lifestyle and diet changes, helping to relieve symptoms and treat the overall condition.

• Fasting improves mental alertness — when toxins are cleared out of the lymphatic system and blood stream, it improves mental clarity. Eating less can result in energy conservation, which can be used by the brain for thinking tasks. In short, fasting is beneficial in the following ways.

• Weight loss
• Improved mental clarity
• Improved breathing
• Improved energy levels
• Better complexion
• Rejuvenated digestive system

SPIRITUALITY AND FASTING

Those who observe religious fasting believe they derive a double benefit, both physical and spiritual, from the practice. Perhaps the benefits of fasting have been experienced since time immemorial, which is why major religions have regularly indulged in fasting as a spiritual discipline and as an aid to devotional practice. The regimen could include juice fasting, liquid fasting, abstinence from meat and from whole meals for varying periods depending on the religion and the practitioner. Christianity encourages fasting during the Lenten season and Judaism during Yom Kippur. Fasting is a sign of repentance, commemorative mourning and gratitude. It is also used to establish self-mastery of spirit over body. By the way, fasting is a predominantly *sattvic* activity.

Fasting is an integral part of Hinduism and generally varies from eating only one meal during the day to refraining from taking food and water for 48 hours. Fasting for a month during the holy month of Ramadan is mandatory in Islam. Fasting in all religions promotes a sense of brotherhood and solidarity. When one goes hungry there is a greater awareness of how our needy and hungry brothers and sisters suffer from want.

Be sure to remember that it is imperative to consult a specialist before embarking on a fast. A specialist usually conducts a thorough medical examination and may even recommend certain diagnostic tests to ascertain if fasting is safe with respect to the patient. Given the medical clearance, a fasting program supervised by a health expert can benefit your health dramatically.

Undoubtedly, fasting is a great way to kick-start the body's self-healing properties into action and enjoy the blessing of good health, increased clarity, insight and receptivity.

THE ELEVENTH DAY

In India there is a monthly fast observance called *ekadasi,* which means the eleventh day. Twice a month on the eleventh day of the waxing and waning fortnight of the moon millions of people observe this simple yet beneficial fast. Ancient texts explain that on the days of *ekadasi* an astrological configuration takes place that is favorable for spiritual awakening and increased health. According to yogic tradition, an unhealthy *tamasic* quality is present in all types of grains on this day. *Tamas* can be a form of decay, which is the opposite of living abundant flow, and therefore it is recommended as a fast day from grains. Beyond this conception is a higher idea that on this day great spiritual merit is accrued by those who fast and increase devotional activities like rendering service to saints, praying, singing the sacred songs, offering charity, temple worship etc. All of these activities are of the nature of *shuddha-sattva* or purified goodness and are therefore very beneficial for body, mind and soul.

The Vedic scriptures describe that *ekadasi* is a favorable time when love between the individual consciousness and the greater consciousness of Divinity has greater abundant flow and therefore its a good time to draw down divine grace and mercy from the infinite abundance of divinity's love for us. Its as if a window is opened in heaven. It is described as a time that is auspicious and favorable for the revelation of abundant grace.

The Vedic conception of Divinity is an all-attractive and all-satisfying transcendental reality personified as a beautiful youth. This is personified historically and mythologically in the character of Shri Krishna, the playful transcendental divine youth who spoke the *Bhagavad-gita* (*Song of God*). Krishna is the Godhead in human form, the spiritual One who is the conscious divine source of all, in His all-pervading aspect as Vishnu. Shri Krishna is the beautiful, all inspiring autocrat whom attracts all, and satisfies all through loving exchange of spiritual *rasa* or emotion. In Sanskrit the name Krishna embodies this concept most completely, and the ideal of Krishna is adored and worshipped by nearly a billion Hindus worldwide. Everyone is drawn to serve the beauty of Divinity through love, just as water naturally flows to the sea. All souls are attracted to the sacred center, which according to theistic traditions is ultimately a transcendentally beautiful spiritual person, the Absolute Reality, reality the beautiful. The Vedas describe that incomparable spiritual beauty as our origin and our fulfillment.

Just as we are naturally drawn to the beauty of a child, our hearts also spontaneously seek fulfillment in our union with Divinity. We don't need to be told to love a child. It's an automatic response of our heart. Similarly, our souls thirst for divine love, ecstasy and self-giving, in other words, reciprocal loving exchanges in a similar almost automatic way. These reciprocal selfless loving exchanges are perfected when our hearts are turned to the love of Godhead. This is called *seva,* or devotional service, and is the primary practice of Bhakti-yoga, the yoga of devotional love.

From the saints and sadhus, and the great spiritual traditions of the world, we are told that what is reciprocated in devotion to us from the absolute side is beyond measurement or calculation. It is absolute good. Reality the beautiful is a conception of divinity as the personified emporium of all loving exchange, and a delightful, playful, divine loving exchange. Our souls naturally love, and our love is perfected when given to our source in divinity. This could be considered the apex of the spiritual conception. If we look at the variety of religious systems in the world, this could be said to be the essence of them all, regardless of cultural or racial trappings.

Observing a fast on this day of *ekadasi* is also an opportunity to heal, cleanse and tone our bodies. It's a natural tune-up that will keep up your vitality. It's also a great way to express the aspiration to love your sacred source, to heal the planet and increase your overall health and well-being. It's another key component to abundance consciousness and abundant living. Like the saying goes *"When you have your health, you have everything."* Abundant health is truly abundant wealth. You can safeguard this wealth with a balanced diet and lifestyle, optimism, faith, piety and a charitable heart.

HABITS CAN HARM OR HEAL

In an article in the Archives of Internal Medicine by Lindsey Tanner, Chicago AP Medical Writer, she states that new research suggests that four common bad habits combined — namely, smoking, drinking too much, inactivity and poor diet, can age you by 12 years. The findings are from a study that tracked nearly 5,000 British adults for 20 years, and they highlight yet another reason to adopt a healthier lifestyle. "The risky behaviors were: smoking tobacco; downing more than three alcoholic drinks per day for men and more than two daily for women; getting less than two hours of physical activity per week; and eating fruits and vegetables fewer than three times daily. These habits combined substantially to increase the risk of death of both men and women, and made people who engaged in them seem 12 years older than people in the healthiest group, said lead researcher Elisabeth Kvaavik of the University of Oslo."

The healthiest group included never-smokers and those who had quit; teetotalers, women who had fewer than two drinks daily and men who had fewer than three; those who got at least two hours of physical activity weekly; and those who ate fruits and vegetables at least three times daily. "You don't need to be extreme" to be in the healthy category, Kvaavik said. "These behaviors add up, so together it's quite good. It should be possible for most people to manage to do it." The U.S. government generally recommends at least 4 cups of fruits or vegetables daily for adults, depending on age and activity level; and about 2 1/2 hours of exercise weekly.

All the evidence of medical science and psychology point to the holistic conclusion that the mind and body are constantly affecting each other in varied and dynamic ways. For a more abundant and healthy life it's essential to develop a cleansing diet and habits of mental and physical exercise. My wife's parents lived way into their eighties and maintained robust health to the end by taking vigorous daily walks. They lived in a small village called Northwood just north of central London and every day they would walk from their home in the Roughs several miles into the village of Northwood and back. They truly enjoyed these walks and it reflected in their overall health and attitudes. They made exercise a fun and rewarding part of their life and as a result they never had to think about it. It was just an integrated aspect of their lifestyle.

You can also make beneficial adjustments to your health and consciousness by incorporating a clean diet, an upbeat attitude and learning to manage your physical and emotional energies. It's really how you frame things in your mind that makes all the difference. Life is an inside job all the way and when your physical organism is performing at optimum levels you'll find that your receptivity to abundant living will take a quantum leap for the better.

VEGETARIAN DIET

The oldest lady in the world was a Russian who died at the age of 120 years. This was one of the interesting news items recently published in a leading national newspaper. There was one characteristic about her life that was peculiar — she was a vegetarian. A vegetarian diet is another key component in increasing your optimal health, receptivity, energy and abundance. Lets look at the facts. Vegetarians tend to live longer and as a demographic group, tend towards healthier lifestyles because someone who cares enough about themselves to regulate their diet will invariably be involved in or interested in the related fields of healing, exercise, meditation and personal growth. Besides, these days being a vegetarian requires no more effort or inconvenience than being a meat-eater. However the benefits of a vegetarian diet are enormous, especially when compared to the damaging effects of a meat-based diet.

Nature has basically created two types of animals — vegetarian and carnivores. The human body is more naturally adapted to vegetarian food than to meat eating. There are a number of facts which prove that nature has made human beings to predominantly eat vegetables and grains, not meat.

1. All meat-eating animals have a very short intestinal tract, only three times the length of their body so that rapidly decaying meat can pass out quickly. In contrast all human beings and

other vegetarian animals have long intestinal tracts, twelve times the length of their body, which is ideally suited to the slow digestion of vegetables and fruits. When an organism with a long digestive tract meant to slowly digest a vegetarian diet eats meat, the meat putrefies in the intestines before it has a chance to be eliminated as it does in the body of a natural carnivore. This putrefication leads to diseases like colon cancer and a host of other diseases.

2. The stomachs of meat-eating animals have large amounts of hydrochloric acid that is needed to digest the flesh. In contrast, the hydrochloric acid content of human beings is 1/10th that of meat eating animals.

3. The salivary glands of meat-eating animals are poorly developed and their saliva is acidic whereas the salivary glands in vegetarians are well developed and saliva is alkaline in nature. It also contains the enzyme ptyalin, which is needed for the digestion of grains.

4. The teeth of non-vegetarian animals are sharp and the canines are well developed to tear flesh. They have no molar teeth and have claws. Vegetarians have flat back molar teeth to grind food and they lack pointed front teeth and the claws of carnivorous animals.

5. All meat-eating animals drink liquids by a licking action of the tongue while human beings drink liquids by joining the lips like most vegetarian animals do. This clearly shows that the human anatomy and digestive system is specifically adapted to live predominantly on fruits, nuts, grains and vegetables. All evidences show that nature has made human beings to predominantly eat grains, vegetables, nuts and fruits.

WHAT IS MEAT?

Meat is the dead carcass of an animal that has most likely been raised in unhealthy factory farming conditions and slaughtered for commercial gain. In reality, meat is not a proper foodstuff for human beings. Yes, in certain circumstances it can sustain and even nourish us. Yet eaten on a daily basis, it becomes poison to the individual and the society. You see, when we reduce other living beings to mere commodities whose lives are worth less than the meat on their backs we psychologically devalue life as a whole. How can we realize a more abundant and peaceful life if we are participating in a lifestyle that denies life to another? It's the opposite of generosity. It's cruelty, it's selfishness, and it's unhealthy, psychologically and physically.

When an animal is killed, fear and violence are energetically embedded in their muscle and tissue. If I consume that meat I absorb that subtle violence into my own system. It's really common sense. I mean, think about it. If we truly want to see an end to violence in America and the world we need to take a hard look at what we're putting into our mouths as well as our minds. It could be argued that people who watch vast amounts of violent video may eventually manifest aggressive tendencies. People who eat meat as a predominant part of their diet suffer the same fate in varying degrees.

Also if we consider the law of *cause and effect*, that every action has an equal and opposite reaction we will understand that if we are involving ourselves in any form of violence we are actually inviting more violence into our lives. It's common sense, not exotic Eastern philosophy. Karma, or action and reaction, is not a myth. Karma is a verified, proven, scientific fact. It was Sir Isaac Newton who said, "For every action there is an equal and opposite reaction," and we witness its operation at every moment of our lives. The ancient sages of the East knew it thousands of years ago. Medical science knows it now and you should know it too. If you throw a ball against a wall, it will bounce back. *Action and reaction. Stimulus and response. This is karma.* If you consume foods that require violence for their manufacture, a degree of that violence will eventually surface in your life either as psychological disturbance or physical disease. As a whole, society suffers when individuals suffer.

I assure you, if you begin to adopt a healthier non-violent vegetarian diet you will come to appreciate a whole new world of abundant food choices, as well as greater mental clarity. The absence of decomposing meat in your system will also help safeguard your health by preventing cancer and a host of other diseases. You will also find your subtle intuitive capacities becoming more refined as well. Qualities like compassion, kindness and deeper insight will arise in your nature, and your mind will brighten as your abilities to read energetic patterns will become more acute. In light of the violent tragedies we repeatedly witness in America, isn't it time we take a closer look at the quality of things we put in our mouths and minds? For a more peaceful world, each of us has a responsibility to become more peaceful within ourselves. A vegetarian diet is a big step towards a more peaceful abundant world. When individuals are peaceful, the society is peaceful. When there is peace, there will also be prosperity.

GLUTEN AS A MEAT ALTERNATIVE

In our family we make a delicious alternative to meat using wheat gluten flour. Here's how we do it. First, purchase some wheat gluten flour from your local health food market. Most local health foods and some bigger stores like Market of Choice carry it in the bins near other types of flour and grains.

Next, put on your favorite music. I like to play some good classical music or an uplifting devotional *kirtan* to set up a happy or spiritual frame of mind. As you cook over heat or fire your thoughts enter the preparation and subtly affect those whom eat your preparations, so it's important to be in a good frame of mind and put love and positive intentions into the food you prepare for your family. *This subtle psychic ingredient of loving-kindness we energetically add to our food preparation is the most important ingredient for health and happiness.*

Take a good size pot and put some olive oil or sesame oil in the pot, perhaps a few tablespoons, and then slowly pour in your gluten flour. You may want to add a few spices at this point as well, like dill, oregano, soy sauce or salt. Next, very slowly, slowly, add water as you mix it by hand gradually kneading it into a big wet doughy mass. It makes a mess of the pot if you let it dry on there, so knead all the excess bits up with the loaf, and quickly wash the pot when you're done kneading it. Then put the gluten loaf on a cutting board and slice it up in thin strips or chunks. Sometimes its easier to use a sharp pair of scissors to snip off small pieces and drop them in a good size pot of boiling water. I usually use the pot that I mixed the powder in, that way I clean the pot as well. The chunks then expand substantially in the boiling water and after boiling them for about 10 to 20 minutes, strain them in a big colander and put them in another pot of cold water to cool them down.

At this point you strain and cool the chunks and slice them up to smaller chunks or thin strips on your cutting board and fry them in a non-stick pan with sesame oil adding more of your favorite spices until they get a bit crispy and pour them into a bowl and sprinkle brewers yeast over them. Alternatively, you can bake them in the oven at 350 degrees for 20 minutes sprinkling more spices and seasonings over them. They go great with basmati rice, salad, all types of dressings, savory sauces and steamed vegetables. They are also a delicious source of protein. There's no fat and they are vegan. Don't forget to say your favorite prayer over your meal and offer it up to the Divine with gratitude and thanks. Then it will nourish your soul as well as your body!

RECEPTIVITY OF THE SPIRIT

It's been my personal experience that if you really want to activate the abundant energetic flow in your life its necessary to realize that the true energetic source of all manifestations is spirit or consciousness. Everything material and spiritual comes from the One Divine source of all abundance. The best way to align oneself with the sacred source of all abundance is through the practice of humility, tolerance and respect for others. The world's various races, religions and cultures all have their unique flavor of approach to Divinity or the Godhead, and this merely reflects the beautiful variety of life and the many ways we can love each other and give recognition to our spiritual source. Spiritual groups may differ in methodology, but it is gross ignorance to demean another cultural or religious approach simply because it differs from our own.

Many paths lead to the mountain. The plurality of religious conception merely reflects the many types, levels, and flavors of human consciousness. Find what resonates with your own heart and unique level of conscious development.

If you want to learn how to love God or Truth or Spirit then first learn how to love his creatures, people and creation unconditionally. If you truly love those whom love God, and whom God loves, you can call off your search for Truth because God will come looking for you. With an open heart and mind you will begin to see Divinity everywhere, in everyone and everything, a unified vision of spiritual cognition. This is *sudarshan,* or *"auspiscious seeing," a* spiritually beneficial and optimistic attitude towards all of life.

God is everlasting abundance, unlimited abundant potentiality and resourcefulness. If you draw affection from the sacred source of the Great Spirit of Divinity you will be in touch with the infinite wellspring of all abundance and goodness. One of the best ways to naturally connect with your own spiritual core and the energetic conscious presence of divinity is to spend quality time in the abundance of nature. Because nature is predominated by the mode of goodness, *sattva-guna*. Nature has a most refreshing effect upon our minds and emotions, unless we drag all of our emotional baggage there too!

So many times I've passed people on the trails in some magnificent primal forest and overheard them ranting on and on about their problems and this and that, and I marveled at how some people can pass through such a magical and beautiful forest and chew on so much internal garbage instead of taking in all of the abundant natural goodness that surrounds them. It's like those people who go camping in a pristine wilderness and bring along a stereo that blasts loud mundane and obnoxious music. They are missing out on a profound source of nourishment and abundance. The best way to experience nature is in the practice I call, *Feeling the Forest*. Empty yourself of all your ideas of yourself and your issues and allow the natural energy of the environment to wash over you, penetrate you, and envelope you in its goodness. Breathe deeply. Get out of your head and into your receptive feelings. Release all tension and mental preoccupations, and allow your body to be cleansed, healed and made whole again by the abundant healthy energy of nature. Something as simple as a quiet walk can become a profound moment of insight, healing and inner unity.

TRANSFORMATION IS THE GOAL

Tukaram was a South Indian saint of renown who lived about five hundred years ago. He had been initiated into the devotional practice of chanting of the holy names of God by Chaitanya Mahaprabhu, the *bhakti-avatar* who traveled throughout India singing God's Holy Names in the fourteenth century, creating a great renaissance of devotional interest. Because of Tukaram's devotional sincerity, his fame spread far and wide. Once, some local villagers were preparing to go on pilgrimage to various holy sites and requested the saint to accompany them. The saint was unable to join them at that time and, after thanking them for their kind invitation, made a strange request of them. He said, "My friends, I am unable to go just now, but please take this bitter melon with you on your pilgrimage, carry it with you throughout your journey, and whether you are walking, resting, or worshiping in the temples, or even while you are taking bath in the holy rivers — always keep it with you." Some of the pilgrims looked at one another with a puzzled look, thinking the request to be a bit eccentric, but knowing him to be a saint they respected his wish.

The pilgrims obeyed the request of the saint and faithfully carried the bitter gourd wherever they went. Taking turns, they carried it to every temple, and also submerged it in every holy river. After several months had passed, the pilgrims returned to the village of the saint and gave him back the bitter melon. With a smile he invited all the pilgrims to a feast to celebrate the completion of their pilgrimage.

The saint then made a special preparation from the bitter melon that had been carried by the pilgrims; as they all sat in a circle, he served it out to them. But as soon as they tasted the bitter melon preparation, they began to complain about its strong bitter taste. In wonder they asked the saint, "Why have you served us this terribly bitter and unripe melon?" As if surprised, the saint replied, "O friends, this melon has been to all the temples and holy places, and has been dipped in all the sacred rivers; how can any bitterness remain within it?" The pilgrims then realized the purpose behind the saint's actions. The saint then said, "It is not enough to simply carry one's body to various holy places yet all the while remaining unchanged within. Nor does the experience of the eyes constitute the realization of truth. When visiting a holy place, one must seek out the saints who reside there and take beneficial instructions from those holy persons. This is the true meaning of pilgrimage." In the ancient book of knowledge called the *Bhagavad-gita* there is a passage in the fourth chapter that states:

"You will attain knowledge of the truth by satisfying those who are situated in that knowledge. Offer your respects to them, and inquire from them submissively. By rendering service unto them, they shall be pleased to impart unto you all the truths which they have realized."

In other words, be receptive and hear from an authority in the field of your interest. This is the fast track to wisdom. There are many ways to induce receptivity and you should explore them all and find what works best for you. Whatever system or practice you adopt, be sure to allow yourself to enter a relaxed and light frame of mind. Bypass the critical factor of the reasoning mind and allow your energy to flow smoothly and evenly through your body. With practice you will gain greater receptivity to the Absolute Abundance of the Universe. Your quality of life will be dramatically enhanced, as well as your perception, understanding and abundance.

REVEAL YOURSELF IN RECEPTIVITY

Have you ever noticed that the boundary to your freedom to love is the boundary to what you can accept in others? If we are to evolve towards peace and fulfillment its helpful to bring attention to the part of you that stands between you and unconditional love. Vulnerability is the gateway to authentic spiritual realization.

Its amazing how often we are afraid to share our authentic self with others for fear of rejection. But if we were to take that leap of faith and reveal our vulnerabilities we would be delighted to realize that others love us far more dearly than they could ever love the false representations that we maintain out of pride, fear or competitiveness. We have to take off our armor to let in love, and to give our hearts to others which is what we all really want. This is why Chaitanya Deva recommended the process of allowing yourself to live in vulnerability when he said: *trnad api sunicena taror api sahisnuna. "Be as humble as the grass and as tolerant as a tree."* Being humble and tolerant and giving honor to others opens us to vulnerability and paradoxically to Divine Grace.

The great apostle of peace Mahatma Gandhi once said: *"Be the change you want to see in the world."* It's a profoundly beautiful statement, but just how does one go about bringing such change to ones life? One possible avenue is to bring awareness to our judgements of others. Leaving aside aversive judgements of others opens the door to greater acceptance of our selves so that healing can take place. We've often heard that when it comes to disagreements its better to be kind than to be right. But we have a great aversion to being rejected which is connected to many thousands of years of tribal life where acceptance in the group meant survival. However we are now at an evolutionary crossroads where large numbers of humanity are waking up to inner evolutionary models. We are all being called to bring more awareness to the aspects of ourselves that cause emotional division and distance from our loving connection to others.

When the Soul of the Whole shines through your mind and intelligence it is wisdom. When it shines through your heart it is unconditional love. When it shines through your actions it is self sacrificing service for the welfare of others. Search out the Soul of the Whole and be a transparent window to let the light out. Open your heart in receptivity, and release yourself from previous conditioning. By discovering your compassionate heart you will realize healing for yourself and better relations with others. What you cannot express controls you in ways you are unaware of. Open your heart to love.

CHAPTER THREE
IDEAL & ACTION

"The key to every man is his thought. Sturdy and defying though he look, he has a helm which he obeys, which is the idea after which all his facts are classified"
—Raplh Waldo Emerson

CREATE YOUR IDEAL

One of the first steps in creating a new and inspiring life, is to create a new and inspiring ideal, by harnessing the great power of imagination. Albert Einstein said, *"Imagination is more important than knowledge,"* and he was absolutely right.

History and human experience demonstrate that cultures that celebrate the imagination and the creative products of imagination are far healthier and more content than cultures that suppress the imagination and its corresponding creativity. Creativity and its source, the imagination, infuse our human experience with a very necessary and dynamic vitality that is enriching to the society and individuals as well. For many centuries Western peoples have maintained a strangely dualistic relationship with imagination, regarding it on the one had as insubstantial fantasy, while all the while almost unconsciously acknowledging it as the source of all developments. We devalue "fairy tales" on one hand and praise creativity on the other, but in reality they have the same origin in the imagination. Our culture places a great deal of emphasis on hard work and realistic thinking. Yet consciousness and imagination are the true creative center of our being from which all new experience are born. Action plays a supporting role in manifestation but imagination is the true creative and unlimited source. Everything we enjoy today began as an idea somewhere in someone's creative imagination. It is the artists, the poets, the mystics and the dreamers that are the true leaders of society. By using the unlimited power of your creative imagination you join the ranks of a very illustrious line of creative and powerful individuals that have brought forth all of the wonderful advances in spirituality, psychology, healing and the arts. No matter who you are, how old you are, or where you are, you also have that creative power within you.

AWARENESS and ASSESMENT

You can begin to release this great creative power by first intentionally dismantling the barriers to what you think is possible. Just for a moment, permit yourself the possibility of unlimited possibilities. Try this experiment. Temporarily suspend your judgment of who you are and what you think is achievable. Allow yourself the freedom to think big, but in a practical way. You want to manifest a more interesting and abundant life? Fine! Just do it with an awareness of your current abilities, interests and resources, and mentally expand those capabilities with creative imagination. It's great to think big but do it in a way that chunks it down into attainable bite-size units. If you're planning to write a book, then begin using your creative imagination to realize the whole book, then break it up into chapters. Create all the main characters, the main scenes, themes and story lines. Work out the inner core of the story line and its procession through conflict and resolution. Make it real, in living color. Hear the voices, feel the emotion of the characters. In other words, bring it to life in the unlimited theater of your own creative imagination. A vision and imaginative process as compelling as this will move great forces in your creative unconscious. In fact, I truly believe that 90% of manifestation is in the creative imaginative process.

PRESENT TENSE

Another critical factor is to see the whole process in present tense. As you develop your ideal or goal and become aware of your current energetic assets, you can also begin to visualize what you will have to do and face in order to reach the point where you are the person who has realized and manifested the goal. Remember, every action has an equal and opposite reaction. So as you move towards your goal by applying realistic and measurable efforts every day you will see the opposites of your efforts also manifesting. Don't be alarmed by this or give into the negative thinking or apathy that may come up. This is normal and easily understandable and if you expect the appearance of these shadows and deal with them you'll pass them by in no time at all. It's a creative process of thesis, antithesis and synthesis.

RISE TO A HIGHER VIEW

Remember, we're looking at the big picture here. The materially conditioned mind cannot solve a materially condition problem. In order to gain greater command of our inner states and empower them for the visualization of a greater goal, we must rise to a higher viewpoint, above our conditioned thinking processes. It is this higher awareness that liberates your intuitive intelligence. We can begin by seeing the golden rail of your aspiration and its shadow, the opposite, the dark rail of energetic apathy, fear of success and other related negativities simultaneously. Think of these two rails as the *ying and yang* of your journey. We live in a dualistic universe. Light and dark, high and low. Pleasure and pain. You can effectively use the knowledge of this polarity to keep your goal and aspirations energetically moving upon these two rails towards manifestation. The dark rail and negativities that come up can also be used as a negative motivator. That is, you can get just as pumped up and excited about your goal from negative resistance as the positive inspiration if you keep a higher view of the whole process by remembering that, *"Success is little more than the ability to take consistent action."* My teacher in India, Srila Sridhar Maharaja, once told me that life is like riding a bicycle, you have to keep pedaling to stay on course and achieve your destination. Negative reactions are nothing more than the shadow of your positive actions. Bigger challenges mean that you're moving towards bigger outcomes if you always keep moving, and remember that *"All of my experiences have positive outcomes."* This isn't wishful thinking, its self-empowering knowledge when you think it, feel it and live it with a generous gratitude before it happens.

STAY ON COURSE

Let me give you another example. Did you know that an airplane flying from San Francisco to New York is off course 90% of the time? Sounds odd doesn't it? But think about it. The plane is veering off course...the pilot corrects...veering off course...the pilot corrects. You do this everyday when you drive your car. Your car doesn't steer itself. What you're doing is making a series of micro-corrections over and over again as you steer down the road. Accidents happen when we don't pay attention to this process, like when we're distracted or impaired as in the case of drunk driving.

So, negativity, apathy or obstacles need have no affect upon your forward movement and can be rendered powerless, or better yet, as a *"left-handed inspiration"* if you have a higher overview of the whole process. It also helps to remember that absolute abundance means you're looking for value in every situation and your eyes are tinged with gratitude for the opportunity to do so. According to Dr. Maxwell Maltz, who wrote the seminal book *Psycho-Cybernetics*, the mind is a goal-striving mechanism. It's important that you utilize your mind as an ally not an adversary. In the ancient literature of India called the *Bhagavad-gita* it is similarly stated:

"The mind is either the friend or the enemy of the living entity."

and in another passage,

"The non-permanent appearances of happiness and distress are like the appearance of winter and summer seasons; they arise from sense perception and one must learn to tolerate them."

Our very own sense perceptions are the cause of our experiencing both happiness and distress, and mind is the perceptive medium. We must use this powerful tool of the mind correctly and to our benefit. Be sure to make your mind your very best friend. In order to do so, you will need to gain a degree of self-unity and self-mastery. Then you will have your hand firmly on the inner controls. Without this inner command you will be pushed and pulled by your impulses, thoughts and emotions. If you think it's easy, just try fasting for a day or two and see how difficult these impulses can be. Self-mastery requires willpower and patience. At the outset it appears difficult, but like any skill, when practiced diligently, strength and skill soon come and the change of perspective is truly empowering.

J.K. Rowling, the author of the wildly popular Harry Potter books, is one of the wealthiest women in the world, perhaps more wealthy than the queen of England. She recently lost her status as a billionaire because she has given away so much of her wealth to charity. She is wealthy as well as wise. The enormous wealth she has generated has benefitted thousands throughout the world, and that wealth has emerged directly from her vast creative imaginative process. With clarity and obsession she wrote it all down. I encourage you to do the same. Get a clear picture in your heart and mind and clarify your vision through creative imagination. Write it out on paper; this will help set your energies in motion.

THE TURNING POINT

Now comes the part that many people have the most difficulty with. Applying consistent action in direct support of the creative imagination. Sometimes it's hard to light a fire under our dreams. This is precisely why a truly compelling inner vision born of creative imagination is so important. Your enthusiasm and emotional involvement is what gives your dreams and ideas the rocket fuel to blast off into physical reality. This is also the reason why it's so critically important to get really clear about what you want. A clear, compelling and creative vision are the first stages of creative lift-off, which must precede what I call the *"turning point factor."* This is where most of us lose it. Whenever I have a new idea I make it a point to write it down or if I can't physically do that in the moment, I make a mental book mark or association that will remind me of it later. Making daily action lists is a proven method of success. In the daily operation of my sign business I write a list of all of the important tasks that need completion on any particular day and work my way down the list. What doesn't get done on Monday gets rolled over to Tuesday. You get the idea.

It keeps me organized and on track. Some days are more challenging than others and there are often interruptions as I'm working down my list, but they are often beneficial as in the case of phone calls from new customers, rush jobs, new opportunities etc.

The *"turning point factor"* is a proper assessment of what to do next with this clear and compelling creative vision. To put it simply, it's an assessment and implementation of what I need to do on a monthly, weekly, daily and momentary level to continue to move my creative imaginative energy towards manifestation. If you're writing a book, you need to write everyday for a set amount of time. Here is consistent action in practice. You don't have to get totally hung up on whether you produce great results every single day, but consistency of practice is crucial. One of the last things my teacher in India said to me was, *"Little drops make an ocean."*

I like to play music. On any given day I usually play sitar, ukulele and sometimes flute. Sometimes I'll play for a few hours in the late afternoon, but often I'll just pick up the instrument for a few minutes. When you are practicing a musical instrument you need to be consistently involved. For me, that means I keep my instrument hanging in my office, and I play, touch or at least look at it every single day. That way it becomes a dynamic interactive part of my daily conscious awareness. I'm emotionally involved with my sitar, and if I don't give her some attention everyday I feel her loneliness.

So get in touch with your creative imaginative process by identifying and clarifying what it is. Back it up with an obsession to write it all down. In some way bring it into the realm of tangible, measurable physical experience.

EMOTIONAL CONGRUENCY

I just wanted to briefly return to the idea of your emotional congruency because it is the fuel that sets all of these processes we have been discussing in motion.

Congruence is the state achieved by coming together, the state of agreement. The Latin *congruere* means *"to come together"* or agree. As an abstract term, congruence means similarity between objects. Congruence, as opposed to equivalence or approximation, is a relation which implies a *kind* of equivalence, though not complete equivalence.

To me, congruence means the focus and unity of energies. By unifying your physical, emotional and mental energies you unite all of your personal power into a concentrated beam of intention. That's personal power you can use.

It was Emerson who said: *"Nothing great was ever achieved without enthusiasm."* To *enthuse,* means to be filled with inspiration, and inspiration is power, it's rocket-fuel, focused, concentrated, and abundant.

If you put your goal into present tense with emotional congruity, enthusiasm and consistent action you become an empowered force that's unstoppable. Emotion is the motion that powers action and if you see yourself living the outcome of your goal in the present tense you literally program your unconscious mind to attract towards you all the people and circumstances that support the manifestation of your realized goal or outcome. But it's got to be real and alive and specific and measurable in your mind and emotions right now, in the present tense.

Don't just weakly affirm, *"I'd like more money."* Or *"I want to be rich."* That's not specific, defined or measurable. Be realistic, and formulate your ideal with the power of measurable action. If you're making $3000.00 a month, say to yourself, *"I am gratefully making another $2000.00,"* and begin looking at your time and resources to see how you can manage them in such a way that you will bring about measurable results. Often it's a simple matter of time management. Little drops make an ocean.

In the day-to-day operation of my sign company I bill my labor time at $55.00 an hour. I'm a person who loves art and the creative process in general, and because of this, on most days I would rather spend my mornings engaged in spiritual activities as well as one of my other interests like playing music, writing or other similarly inspiring pursuits. My workdays usually begin around noon or 1pm and working like this I enjoy a relaxed creative lifestyle. Most days I only work for four or five hours at the most. Some would call that semi-retired, and I'm grateful for the leisure time I enjoy. My income averages between $35,000 to 45,000 a year. Some might consider it ludicrous for a man of my income to write a book about abundance. But abundance isn't really about material acquisition; it's about consciousness and attitude.

Once I looked at my income, productivity and number of hours available on any given day, and realized that if I increased my productive hours (notice I didn't say work, because I love what I do. My work is also part of my creative process) by 25% my income would rise up $14,300 to $59,300.00 annually. This I have actually done, however, working more than this cuts too far into my creative time, and therefore I generally enjoy my life at an easier pace. However, if I were to double the amount of productive sign hours in a day, a week and a month, my income could potentially shoot up to $90,000!

Just a small adjustment of 25% more daily time invested on my part, brought my income up from $45,000 to $60,000 and a 50% increase of my involvement with a commercially lucrative creative process that I enjoy and which also provides a valuable service to others would potentially raise my income to nearly $100,000 a year! Remarkably, I could still have time in the early mornings, evenings and weekends to enjoy my family and the various creative processes that are part of my life. *Work smarter, not harder*, is an old saying that still rings true. It's what I tell my children, along with the recommendation that they go into business for themselves. You can also put added positive energy behind these ideas by mentally dedicating a portion of your increased income for the benefit of others through charity and other forms of giving.

This is an example of a realistic goal with measurable progress taking shape through consistent daily action. You can do this as well. Take stock of your current position and opportunities and multiply your efforts by 25% in any area and look how much you can economically grow by just this small step. Another secret to all of this is that as soon as you stretch yourself a little bit, it becomes easier to stretch further. Whatever area you wish to increase, be it physical body or ability in music or another professional skill, stretch and repeat, stretch and repeat. Grow yourself a little further than your current position and apply the law of repetition. Repetition gets results, and repeated results fuel a greater appreciation for results and the actions that support them. It's a living dynamic process of success. Inspiration, action, repetition, inspiration.

ACTION AS EVOLUTION

So you can see that imagination is a powerful tool that you possess right now. For many people it's a vast untapped resource that can be developed with practice, receptivity and flexibility of attitude, belief and action. Remember to write it all down for clarity or create a compelling vision board that depicts you and your family engaged in all the activities you desire to be engaged in, and surrounded by all the items that support your vision. See it now, and work towards its manifistation.

A MORE DYNAMIC VISION BOARD

Most of us spend a lot of time in front of the computer. I work from home, so I use mine quite a bit. I like to collect inspiring pictures from the Internet and drop them into my screensaver folder on my computer. That way these inspiring images are constantly appearing every few minutes on my desktop computer screen reminding me of the beautiful and abundant life I'm currently living. This is very effective because it creates an endlessly changing and inspiring slide show going on in the background of my work day, constantly feeding my subconscious mind all of the images and corresponding feelings that nourish my dreams into manifestation. Try this. I guarantee that in a very short amount of time you'll begin to feel the powerful effect of the screensaver vision board.

Now get some rocket fuel under your dreams by taking focused action everyday. Make daily lists of what you need to do and power through it with enthusiasm. The more you do the more you'll feel like doing. I find it immensely satisfying to power through my list because I know each item I tick off is part of the stream of abundance that supports my growing lifestyle of energetic flow. The more goes out, the more comes in. Movement is life, and action is passion. Passion is enthusiasm, and enthusiasm is faith in motion.

INVOLVED OR EVOLVED

At this point we have to ask ourselves are we involved or evolved? I mean, are we just becoming busier or are we growing into the people we want to be? After all, the whole point of life is to grow, expand and realize. Plants do it, animals do it, and people do it. Even rocks do it in the form of crystals. The universe does it. Look at the big picture....birth, growth, maintenance, creative production, eventual dwindling, decay and disappearance, followed by fresh creative production, birth, growth...You see, a dynamic cyclical flow. Realization of these processes is the best part of our involvement because it leads to *evolvement,* the evolution of our personal and collective consciousness. Growth is abundance in flux. So don't get busy just because you're running from fear, and don't get busy because you're running to pleasure. Get busy because it's the *dharma* of life to move energy. Dynamic energetic flow — this is where the action is. This is the theater of abundant life. Inner evolution is the dynamic realization of abundant flow. By giving to life for the sake of giving, all of our actions have the potential to become *karma-*

yoga, or a linking with the Divine through selfless action. This is inner evolution, and when you're evolving, you are growing and realizing you are in a state of absolute abundance. Finding your *dharma* in life is to find your unique contribution to life. By performing your dharma or particular calling in such a way as to benefit others you will evolve spiritually as well as prosper materially. Whatever is in motion is living and growing. What is inert is stale and decaying.

EX ORIENTE LUX

...a light from the east...

Remember that dynamic excitement of being in school or college when you were truly engaged and enthusiastic about the subject? For me personally, those were the moments when I felt the most enthusiastic about life. I regained that excitement when I began to explore Eastern spirituality more earnestly. I began to seek out higher associations and make connections and associations that would eventually bring out the best in me. I had grown up in a time when the rampant drug experimentation of the 60's and 70's was still residually present. In my high school and college years drug use had become recreational rather than experimental. Pot smoking and alcohol were the norm across all social levels, and parties were regular and excessive. By the time I reached my mid-twenties I was ready to dedicate myself to a higher and healthier lifestyle. As a child I had always been fascinated with Native Americans and foreign cultures in general. I loved National Geographic magazine and one of my favorite programs on T.V. was Mutual of Omaha's Wild Kingdom. I loved animals and exotic cultures and was fascinated by wild indigenous peoples in remote parts of the natural world. I was fascinated by the exotic Far East, travel and exploration.

I longed to travel and experience the world in search of deeper truths. To see and experience the abundance of the world.

It's no wonder I was captivated by the mystery and depth of Tibetan and Indian spiritual traditions. As I researched and read more about the ancient yogic evolutionary models of these cultures, the more I wished to immerse myself in their understanding. I had been reading the ancient Hindu scripture Bhagavad-Gita *(The Song of God)* and found the second chapter most illuminating for it clearly delineated the energetic contrast between conscious spiritual existence and material biological form. It described consciousness as a distinct energy in contrast to earth, water, fire, air and ether. These ideas made sense to me and I had come to a crossroads in my life. It was time for a change, so I began regularly visiting a Krishna temple in Berkeley, even though it was a two-hour drive away.

After sometime I decided that I must find spiritual community and regular association closer to my home so I searched and searched in San Francisco and the East bay, but could not find what I was looking for. Then one day in my desperation while visiting the Berkeley temple I prayed earnestly at the altar of the guru A.C. Bhaktivedanta Swami for guidance. As soon as I exited the temple room a woman asked me who I was and what I was looking for, and when I explained my situation she gave me the phone number of a spiritual community in San Jose which was much closer to where I currently lived at the time.

I knew my prayer had been answered when I first set foot in the San Jose ashram. I could feel the openness, humor and relaxed yet engaging atmosphere that confirmed I was in the presence of like-minded souls, and was on the right path to further growth. Although it was a monastery there was a great sense of humor that lent a sense of family community to the serious dedication of the members. They were extremely generous with their time and knowledge and in a short period of time I made many new friends who shared the same higher ideals of spiritual growth as myself. The directors of the ashram were celibate monks who had taken formal vows of renunciation from material life and wholly dedicated themselves to a lifestyle of purity and service.

The community there was centered on the printing, publishing and distribution of spiritual literature and my skills as a fine artist and graphic arts major put me in good stead. My first project was to decoratively paint the main ashram building with beautiful blue airbrushed lotus blossoms. It was an historic building designed by the famous architect Bernard Maybeck (1862–1957), who was a prominent architect in the Arts and Crafts Movement of the early 20th century. It was a beautiful mansion with redwood interior walls and a majestic spiral staircase.

ACCELERATED LEARNING

After a year of beautifully decorating the ashram building with airbrush paintings I was invited to live full time on the property and it was at this time that my consciousness greatly expanded. I would rise at 4:30 am every day, rain or shine, in sickness or in health, and faithfully attend the morning worship and classes on spiritual philosophy. Then after a hearty breakfast, I would study scripture and memorize Sanskrit passages from the Vedic literatures. I followed this scheduled lifestyle for over two years and the result was dramatic. Hundreds of verses were memorized and due to this great influx of wisdom I felt a great increase of understanding and personal potency. The rest of my day I was engaged in performing various necessary duties with particular emphasis upon graphic arts, book layout, preparing film and plates for the printing press etc. In the evening we would attend another service and class and then take a light meal before bed.

It was this total immersion in a monastic lifestyle with like-minded association that taught me the value of focus and the power of a high ideal backed by congruent action. Within a few short months I felt a dramatic acceleration of consciousness.

I was living a concentrated spiritual lifestyle without any distractions of T.V., radio, parties or involvement with the opposite sex. We were eating pure vegetarian food and abstaining from intoxication as well. It was a monastic situation that effectively separated me from all of my previous distractions and powerfully instilled a dynamic spiritual paradigm, which gave me a greater perspective with which to gauge the relative value of all my experiences. My studies and association with more spiritually mature individuals gave me an expanded sense of possibility both spiritually and materially and greatly enlarged my vocabulary and cognitive abilities far beyond what I had previously thought possible. Eventually I traveled to India several times and was initiated into the priestly brahminical order of Vaishnava traditional culture and began giving classes and conducting outreach programs myself. I'll always be grateful to those early friends, mentors and teachers at the ashram who gave me the understanding and deeper perspective of a greater fulfillment in life and generously opened the doors to my greater understanding.

It was their generosity and friendship that opened the door to greater possibilities of abundant growth. My own receptivity opened up my own doors of perception to receive their light. The combination was heated with my own passionate involvement and the result was total transformation. Ideal and action will bring transformation if you put all of your energy into it, and good association is vital to this process.

SEE THE VALUE NOW

Decisive and active people seize opportunities in the present. They don't wait and calculate what they have to give up in the form of personal time and energy. They see value in the spontaneous and powerful actions of the present. They may or may not have the outward symptoms of wealth like cars, homes and cash. But the real factor is the inner decisive state of mind.

The expanded consciousness of abundant opportunity and energetic flow that will bring more of everything into your life is linked to your ability to take intelligent but decisive action in the present. Procrastination is stagnation, the opposite of dynamic action. It's helpful to remember all the times in your life when you jumped on an opportunity and it paid off in spades. If you can't remember such moments personally, then remember scenes from your favorite adventure books or films when others did what you would like to do. Paste yourself into that picture. Become the hero of your own life. Envision your self as the dynamic and daring individual whom Fortune favors because they bravely take action. If you need source images think of your favorite heroic characters from films or any action or sports hero that inspires you.

Practicing the abundant induction technique and familiarizing yourself with the decisive moods that you most wish to attract into your own energetic flow will do wonders in bringing about a more clearly defined consciousness of abundance in your life. So set your inspiring goal or ideal life in your heart and mind and back it up with consistent and congruent action. First write it down, imagine it and then live it. Your nervous system and the unconscious mind can't tell the difference between a vividly imagined experience and an actual physical experience. Work with these concepts and you'll begin experiencing dramatic results.

Now I'd like to make you aware of another powerful link to greater abundant flow. It's the immense power of relationship, which also includes the allied powers of association and rapport.

CHAPTER FOUR
RELATIONSHIPS

"The most effective way to achieve right relations with any living thing is to look for the best in it, and then help that best into the fullest expression."

-*Anonymous*

IMPORTANCE OF RAPPORT

People are our greatest asset for realizing a more fully abundant life, and rapport is the connecting link. Affection, love and compassion are the inner currencies of this connection, and can greatly increase the energetic flow to this vital area of our lives.

If we feel alienated from others, we are definitely choking the flow of abundance in our lives. Often this is due to attitudes of competitive dualism, bias, prejudice and fear, all of which create distance between individuals and communities. These negative barriers are products of ignorance, and in the deepest sense, this is symptomatic of our spiritual ignorance or lack of insight into the reality of life.

By contrast, a sense of commonality and community strengthens rapport. It's that feeling of unity between individuals and groups of people, the unified sense of purpose and appreciation, that brings us together and opens the lines of communication and opportunity. A strong sense of commonality and community strengthens our rapport. Genuine rapport always brings about a greater feeling of unity between individuals and groups of people. This type of mutual appreciation enhances our feelings of connectedness and the free flow of enhanced appreciation and communication. Through affection, humor, wisdom and genuine appreciation for the good qualities in others we find the currency of success and tap into the flow of absolute abundance. All of these positive qualities are enhanced by genuine spiritual insight and the unbiased wisdom which deeper insight admits to our thoughts and behaviors.

Spiritual wisdom and understanding enhances our compassion and understanding of other people, which in turn gives us a greater skill in managing our own inner states as well as our communications and relations with others.

Wikipedia defines rapport as one of the most important features or characteristics of human interaction. It is a commonality of perspective or being "in sync" with or being "on the same wavelength" as the person with whom you are talking. In other words it's a commonality of energies, interests, thoughts and emotions, which enriches communication. Sometimes, its not so much what you say as how you say it, and we always give precedence to our feelings about someone, regardless of what they may actually be saying. There's an old saying in this regard; *"No one cares how much you know, until they know how much you care."*

Rapport, or lack of it, is often automatic. If rapport is lacking there are a number of techniques that can be beneficially employed in building rapport such as: matching your body language with another through posture, gesture, vocal tonality and expression. Also maintaining eye contact and matching breathing rhythms can be helpful. Many of these techniques are explored in Neuro-linguistic programming but there can be deeper more caring and indeed spiritual ways to build rapport, which enhance a more intimate connection with other people, animals and the environment. Of these, genuine affection, compassion and insight based upon spiritual wisdom and understanding are the best.

Spiritually speaking, people are the true wealth of life. They are more important than ideologies, doctrines and views. People are the living conduits of abundant energetic flow, for every goodness we have experienced in life has come through other people.

Family, friends, teachers, mentors, priests, authors, musicians, mystics and artists have all contributed to the ongoing richness of our lives, and one small act of kindness has been known to change a person's life. One encouraging word from the right person at the right time can sometimes do more to inspire us than years of study. One person, inspired by one act of genuine kindness may go on to affect hundreds or thousands of other people through the processionary effect of their actions. In this simple way, goodness may be multiplied and expanded throughout communities, nations and worlds.

Sometimes we are graced with a lesson through the apparent aggression of others. Often the hardest experiences of our lives are the most beneficial, for wisdom is born of experience, and if we can look deeply into difficult events as teachers, not punishments, our wisdom will grow greatly. All of our interactions with other people give us experience. Some negative experiences can be very empowering for us if we are skillful in our own communications with ourselves and understand the inner methodologies of psychologically transforming inner representations. Many experiences are neutral in nature and others are highly beneficial and life affirming. In the final analysis however, it is our inner perspective that actually determines what value we take away from or give to any experience. Social interaction is opportunity, opportunity that requires a certain degree of courage and honesty to seek out the best. Give the best, and anticipate the best in others as well as yourself. Isolation is stagnation and stagnation is decay, the antithesis of life, growth, movement and abundance.

Every major turning point in my life came or was inspired by another person. I am grateful to all those people who made deposits into the rich tapestry of my life.

In my own experience, I've found the best way to strengthen rapport and unity between myself and others and thereby increase the positive probabilities of life, is to look for commonality with others. Obviously rapport is naturally apparent when we share a common interest with others. If I'm interested in music or art, motorcycle repair or computers...whatever it may be, I will immediately be in rapport with others who share such interests... no brainer there, right?

But what about those people with whom we don't share any apparent interest or commonality? What about those people and ideas that are in opposition to our interests?

How can we find a golden thread of rapport and build it into a solid bridge of stable energetic flow? Well, first of all the best policy is to relax, because nothing makes another person feel at ease as much as when you feel at ease within yourself. Some people are so wound up and so desperate to connect with others that their inner tension and desperation actually drives everyone else away. Neediness can damage rapport unless you're trying to connect with a priest, a nurse or a puppy dog.

DESIRE AND DETACHMENT

Remember that time when you were really attracted to someone and you really didn't want to blow it and that's exactly what you did! You embarrassed yourself by fumbling all over yourself... Yes, we've all done it, and it's related to desire. Of course, in manifesting goals in our life, desire and emotional congruency are the fuel that powers our consistent actions, but it's also equally important to have intelligence and insight at the steering wheel. These qualities impart to us skillfulness in dealing with other people. When the desire is too strong or unbalanced, or immaturely or inappropriately applied we lose perspective. Losing perspective can cause a distortion of intelligence which then leads to unskilled behaviors.

Here's a bit of ancient wisdom for you from the *Bhagavad-Gita*: *"When contemplating the objects of the senses one develops attachment for them. From such attachment great longing arises, from this desire one develops anger, and when anger arises intelligence is lost."*

This passage illustrates how anger can be the little brother of desire. When our desires are frustrated, we lose our intelligent perspective. Even before frustration sets in, at the outset of great burgeoning desire, intelligence is often compromised. *"Falling in love"* is a perfect example.

What do people mean when they "fall in love"? It's a subjective state of heightened attraction for another person wherein our critical factor of intelligence is compromised and the qualities of the other person are greatly magnified and appreciated, often beyond their actual level. In other words, it can be a full-blown distortion of rapport, attraction and desire.

UNREQUITED LOVE

Have you ever "fallen in love" with someone? You know, when you lavish affection upon them, or tried to connect with them but they obviously weren't in the same space as you? Did they look at you like you were crazy? Like, what's this person on about?

For whatever reason, there wasn't the same level of romantic rapport. Perhaps in your romantic enthusiasm you jumped the gun and overstated your feelings before any genuine rapport could be established between the two of you. This will usually scare away another person because they will immediately recognize that you are too preoccupied with your own feelings and that you really don't even know them yet. Your critical factor of intelligence has been compromised by your own over-blown internal representation of the other person. I painfully watched my friend go through this embarrassing progression over a girl he was infatuated with. It was painful to watch as he began to downgrade and criticize himself in the process. Silly isn't it? We create representations in our own minds and then emotionally react to them and disempower ourselves in the process.

Love is the most intoxicating and inspiring force in the universe, but you should approach it wisely. Love and affection have produced great works of art and many inspired deeds. However, I do think its helpful to be more aware of the whole progression and to use it to empower ourselves for greater self awareness, growth and a more joyful abundant life. It should be inspiring not disempowering. Two people fall in love because they have a similar level of emotional and psychological development. Physical attraction often gives sexual-emotional power, but it is the quality of the inner person that counts in the end.

Often couples have great physical and romantic attraction, but as we all know, these relations tend to diminish over time until we arrive at the reality of facing the inner emotional and psychological temperament of our partner. When this happens in a marriage, it's a turning point of great significance. It's the point where you either decide to carry on and grow internally as individuals by supporting each other's growth, or separate and possibly divorce. It typically takes place in the first or second year of marriage. The best marriages have a paradigm of friendship and psychological and emotional compatibility at their core. The added strength of spiritually supportive ideals can make relationships more enduring because the very concept of growing through difficulties as a spiritual path is woven within the very fabric of the relationship. This is another secret of success that is often overlooked in our fast paced modern lives that are increasingly divorced from cultural identities and spiritual ideals.

I once became so infatuated with a girl that I felt a great creative inspiration. It was a period of heightened inspiration that enabled me to produce many songs and music, which marked a creative high point in my life. The greater benefit however, was when I realized that this wonderful heightened sense of being and creativity was entirely my own doing! It was produced by my own internal representations of the woman. She was indeed the catalyst, but the energy and emotion had its origin within my own being. This was a great epiphany for me because I realized I could produce this inner awareness and excitement on demand, and you can too! You have the great power of affection within you. Use it wisely. Direct it. Let it empower you for greater achievement.

Inner distortions can also work their illusion when an individual is so full of him or herself, that they become annoyingly over-confident. It's another negative distortion of perspective and often a symptom of insecurity. Conceit is the only sickness that makes everyone else sick besides the one who's got it. It's a really big rapport killer. Remember, we build rapport and connection with others through similarity and affection. Setting ourselves up as being superior divides us against ourselves as well as others.

INCREASING RAPPORT

To increase rapport first relax and remain detached. If you send out a "needy" vibe then you may only attract other needy persons, or those who will exploit your neediness. Confidence likes confidence and ease creates ease. Like attracts like. Next, ask questions and be open to the natural conversational flow. People love it when another person takes interest in them, even when they pretend not too!

You'll be surprised how much rapport is generated through simple questions and answers if you keep the mood light, friendly and especially humorous. Humor is the best form of rapport because laughter has a delightful way of opening us up emotionally.

I knew a man who had once been convicted of a felony and did time in prison for three years. He told me a humorous story about how he was on a flight and was sitting next to another man who informed my friend he was a high-court judge; my friend replied to the judge, "That's funny because I'm a criminal!" They had an instant and unlikely rapport. They became good friends after this initial meeting. Humor was the link, common experience and affection built the rapport between them.

HANDLING DIFFICULT PEOPLE

The most important thing to understand about people who bother us is that the botheration resides in us, not them, and by dealing primarily with our own responses, we free ourselves of the bother and empower ourselves to behave with greater skill and more compassionate actions.

Whenever two people meet, the one with the most self-control will always be in the superior position. If you encounter difficult people in your day and have the presence of mind to remain centered and undisturbed, eventually they will either come around to your way of thinking or go away. You can remain peaceful, and agree to disagree in a non-adversarial mood, and that will gradually disarm them. They will feel your compassion for them if you are sincere. Humor can also be effectively employed to break their aggressive behavior.

Another important point about difficult people is that often the reason why they are mean or unfriendly is because they are carrying emotional hurt somewhere inside them. When you understand that someone is acting up because they are suffering it's easier to feel compassion for them. When they sense your genuine compassion it will build a bridge of rapport between you if you are careful not to patronize them.

Eventually they will warm up to you in time because they will respect you for not being weak in the face of their aggression, and secondly, when they intuit your compassion towards them they will actually desire your friendship. However, it's important to avoid over-doing it by patronizing them or being overtly sympathetic. Be genuine. Be sincere. Be kind, strong and patient. Control your own responses and you will indirectly control the responses of others. Interestingly, arguing now and then for the right reasons may also be good for your health, and absolutely necessary when needed.

A study by researcher Kira Birditt, of the Institute for Social Research at the University of Michigan found that when people experience tension with someone else, whether their boss, spouse, or child, sidestepping confrontation could be bad for their health. They found that avoiding conflict was associated with more symptoms of physical problems the next day than was experienced by actually engaging in an argument. How we deal with problems can significantly affect our daily well being and health.

The most common way for people to deal with their interpersonal problems is to simply avoid them. Unfortunately no one grows when we avoid confrontation. An underlying affection coupled with a light-hearted humorous approach can lubricate even the most difficult confrontations. You can build rapport with anyone, in any situation, when you become skilled in understanding and directing your own emotional states. When you more clearly understand yourself, you will also more clearly understand others. Most aggressive people try to control others through fear and desire. If you cannot be intimidated or enticed, you will retain your personal power in a remarkable way.

The best quality of rapport is built through genuine affection. Be genuinely kind and you will have very few enemies. After all, the only true enemy is your own uncontrolled mind.

SPIRITUAL RAPPORT

Remember the paradigm of the conscious self we explored in chapter one? It went like this:

In reality, I am a pure point of conscious light,
A conscious awareness without beginning or end.
I am unlimited in my conscious potentiality.
It is my nature to grow and to love.
All beings are of a similar nature.

This philosophic and energetic understanding imparts the spiritual clarity to view all life in a simplified, affectionate and straightforward way. It builds rapport and connection with other people and indeed all species at the deepest level because it represents the deep understanding that we are all here to grow, to love, and to share. Despite the surface appearance of any individual, whatever they look like, whatever their level of success or education, despite the emotional temperament or the inner psychological processes, spiritually, we are all of one similar nature. In this sense, all beings are created equal. Though all are simultaneously unique and special in their own right.

Do you see how empowering this broad view of life is? It builds lasting rapport in friendships, marriages and businesses because it addresses the very core of our inner being. It is unfailing when practiced with sincerity. If I see all living beings with this equality of inner vision and recognize that every being is, like myself, in a dynamic phase of growth, I will be able to accommodate anyone and create rapport with anyone. I will be able to find ways to nourish the hearts of others. We will see true abundance and value in everyone, everywhere and in everything. This is the realization of absolute abundance. It is an unfailing success principle because it is an expression of one of the most fundamental truths of our existence.

Affection is the connection, and spiritual affection is the deepest connection. It's the recognition of eternal value in other living beings and a commitment to foster their growth from whatever their current position into a greater awareness and joy. This is akin to the Bodhisattva vow to compassionately care for the well being of others. If you truly and genuinely care for the well-being of others on the deepest level of consciousness, with concern for their growth and happiness, you will always find rapport and connection and opportunities in the company of others. No matter who they may be.

Five hundred years ago there was a group of six saints who lived in a sacred palace called *Vraja Dham*. They were called the six Goswamis, and it was said that they were "popular with the gentle *and* the ruffians." I always found that interesting. They were popular even with the ruffians! Why? Because they were humble. They were so spiritually advanced that they did not place themselves above others. They were always genuinely concerned for the welfare of others and this endeared them with everyone. *Goswami* is a title meaning, *master of the senses*. They were masters, of their minds, senses and behaviors. They were never bothered by the behavior of others, because they were constantly absorbed in their own inner representations of the divine life. The environment could never disturb them. As a result they were able to skillfully deal with others in a way c´

their own choosing that was always generous and beneficial.

I've had the honor to meet several individuals with these remarkable qualities and their energetic presence is wonderful, unifying and affectionate. They relate to all classes of people because of their authenticity, humility and concern. They are precious. In Tibet they are called *Rinpoche*. You can develop these qualities too, by practicing humility, tolerance and respect for others.

BUSINESS RAPPORT

I am not a recognized authority on business matters. In fact I think I'm business challenged, yet somewhat creatively empowered. However, I do understand human relationships to some degree. I think the quality of our relationships is based on the quality of our communication power. I would also venture to say that quality communications and quality relationships are the very bedrock of consistent and enduring business success. I'm a creative person by nature, and generally relate well with other people. I like to see other people happy. From a traditional point of view this isn't always the best success formula, but interpersonally, I think it's more rewarding.

I recently had an experience that illustrates the great power of rapport and how it opens up the channels of our abundant flow. I'm a commercial sign manufacturer whose primary product is computer-cut, adhesive-backed, vinyl graphics. I often create logos, signs and designs for customers in programs like Adobe Illustrator. Depending upon the final application, I will either digitally print a full color image or vectorize the art (reduce it to outlined art) and cut it on a vinyl plotter which basically cuts the image out much like a stencil, only in this process you weed away the background material leaving the positive image to be applied to a sign substrate, a window, banner or vehicle.
I have a customer that owns a store that specializes in video games and they wanted me to apply their logo to the store window,

which I did. But then I realized that I could build more value into the sale by recommending another logo because their window frontage was so big it made good advertising sense to increase the name visibility with more logos. The customer agreed but later came back and said that she wanted me to remove the first logo and change it to another height. She was apologetic for the confusion and told me it was acceptable for me to add an additional charge to the invoice. But in the interest of building good business rapport (by offering generous service) I told her I wouldn't charge her extra to redo the logo and remove the old one. This impressed her and brightened her mood, at which she replied, that instead of more money she'd give my son a gift certificate for the balance, to which I graciously accepted.

Then we began talking about adding the logo to another window on the opposite side of the building, but the final payoff came when our rapport had peaked, and we felt the comfort and personal ease in our conversation to exchange personal information. At this point I asked her where she worked and she replied at the University of Oregon, which sparked my interest because I'd been attempting to become a vendor providing signs and banners for the University. I knew it would be a lucrative account and boost our sign sales. I mentioned to her that I had recently received an invitation by mail to the University's upcoming Vendor Fair and that I was looking forward to making new business connections there, to which she replied, "Oh my friend is a key figure in the purchasing department there. You need to go directly to him and submit your request form. All vendor requests pass through him." I thought... Jackpot! Here's the connection I've been looking for! Then she said; "I'll be sure and mention your name to him this week."

I was delighted by this development. It really demonstrated that patience and genuine rapport through sincere communication opens so many doors to our abundance. Flexibility made it possible.

Now if I had adopted a negative attitude towards her initial logo changes I would have been grumpy about losing time and materials and wouldn't have been in the positive and open frame of mind to have that sincere conversation which eventually lead to such a powerful business opportunity.

I had another similar experience not long after this one. I received an email from a woman at an art center that needed a banner the very next day for a show. She was desperate and I knew because of time leverage, I could basically *"charge what the market may bear,"* as is often the case with rush jobs. In other words, although I'm in the sign business, *"I could take her to the cleaners"* if I were a more exploitive person. However, I believe it's important to provide good service first and treat customers with generosity and respect. When I called her I was so impressed by her kind mood that I decided that I'm going to build some value into this job. I looked up the price for the 3ft by 15ft banner and saw that the price estimating book for signs said it should sell for $275.00 but I told her I would support the arts and give her a $50.00 discount even though it was a rush job. Well, she was delighted, and after seeing the proof via email she gave me the go ahead. I like to jump on things right away so I promptly cut the vinyl and ordered the blank banner material. No worries...

Then later that night I received a copy of an email forwarded by her superior complaining that she had not had the content of the banner approved by upper management, and that it had to be changed. I really felt for her at this point, and decided that, although I had already cut the lettering I would re-cut it without charging extra. My reasoning was, that first of all, this lady was in a hurry to get this banner for the next day, so she was stressed and she made the common mistake of *"jumping the gun."* Being a passionate person myself, I'm guilty of this sort of behavior all the time, so I could sympathize. Having worked for many years in corporate environments, I know what it's like to order something and then realize that you just wasted the company's money, because in your haste you didn't get it right. Ouch!... embarrassment with corporate superiors!

Secondly I wanted to add value by demonstrating generosity of service. I knew that they would remember the generous way I treated them, and hopefully that would bring them back to me next time they needed another banner for a special event. Call it an advertising investment. Ultimately, I did it because it rang true with my personal and business philosophy that energetic flow must be allowed to happen for greater abundance to be realized. My generous mood opened the door for greater flow, now and in the future. Well, it did bring an immediate return for me because she then offered me a free listing in their directory as a local contributing business that supports the arts. A much bigger value than the $15.00 in vinyl material I *"lost"* by having to re-cut the lettering. Giving is getting in disguise. Sometimes it takes time to show up, which requires patience on our part.

Both of these experiences illustrate that what appears to be a setback at the outset can become a greater benefit at the conclusion. Patience and rapport and sincere communication make it all possible. The way you communicate with others is a big factor in determining the amount and quality of abundance that flows to you, and through you. Be an open door. Be patient. You'll be surprised how creatively events can unfold when we get our egos out of the way. If you're in business, look at your product or service as a streaming energy flow. Look for areas in your own consciousness, emotions and behavior that create blockages to this flow. Whenever business is slow I know its time to give something away. I call it *"priming the pump."* In other words, it's a way to get some flow moving down the energetic pipeline. Take some positive and generous action to get the energy moving. Reach out to others in generosity. Once you've established flow, its only a matter of time before *"what goes around, comes around"* in your direction once again.

THE END OF COMPETITION

By appreciating the symbiotic relationships that all human beings share, your rapport will naturally grow as you realize that helping others gain what they want, you'll always get what you want. In business, this concept builds rapport in every area of personal relations. Whether it be employer and employee, business owner and the public, wholesale supplier and business owner, all will prosper through cooperation and service. It is our inner nature to love and serve that which we love. When you give affection and service to others in a mood of assisting them towards the fulfillment of their need, you will no longer feel the need to compete or compare yourself with others because you will understand that through our united symbiosis there is no lack in this abundant universe. By offering genuine service you will attract more business, more clients, and a better quality of business clientele. You'll often get what you want if you help enough others get what they want.

ASSOCIATION IS A MIRROR

Another important factor in building rapport is to understand the power of association. Association is like a mirror. Whatever we associate with, we reflect in our own nature. As I stated previously, to develop greater command of ourselves it's imperative that we take control of our mental states.

In order to override past conditioning and refresh ourselves with new and more beneficial states, and the more elegant actions that follow, we need to give better quality perceptual input to our minds. Think of it as sowing a garden. The seed-thoughts you place in your mind will grow to produce a sweet or bitter fruit and the thought-seeds we sow in our minds will be colored by the types of associations we share with others.

We mirror the qualities of the people we build a regular rapport with, and as we continue to associate, we will share states of consciousness, thought and behavior. No mystery here.

The type of people you associate with will determine to a great extent the types of energies and attitudes that influence your own behavior. There's a saying *"If you lie down with the dogs, don't be surprised if you get up with fleas."* Through bad association we acquire negative destructive habits of thinking and behavior. Through positive, and especially, higher types of association, we can gain greater skill and understanding. We do this all the time. If you want greater skill in a given area, you go to someone who themselves have that greater skill. Through association and repetition, you also develop that particular skill.

Good, and especially higher association is vital. If we are habituated to negative thinking and unskilled behavior, it's essential that we find better association in the company of more developed and psychologically mature individuals. We want to share quality time with people who share our deep interest in bettering ourselves. Good association always makes a world of difference.

In my own life I saw this first hand when I left the company of my teenage friends who were addicted to drug use. At first I knew I was meant to find a higher way of life, but I wasn't sure which direction to move in, so I simply removed myself from negative association and began studying uplifting and inspiring literatures. Books are wonderful in this regard. However, books are passive agents. Much can be gained from them, but so much more comes from a living agent. So although I was alone, I associated with higher thought through the medium of books. That cleared space in my life for higher energies to flow in. Sometimes we have to bravely go it alone to make room for change. We may have to patiently wait out a seemingly empty period for a while.

After some time I began to visit study groups, ashrams and temples and eventually I had a completely new community of friends who shared the kind of spiritual ideals and lifestyles that inspired me as well. I clearly developed my ideal, took action in that direction with faith, and eventually achieved the positive result. In order to escape negative and unhealthy association we have to call the bluff on our own conditioning and fear. Sometimes we have to end one relationship before we begin another. We may not see the better relationship yet, but by clearing space for it in our emotional and mental lives we invite it, and assure its eventual arrival.

Just as the light of one candle can light many other candles without diminishing its own light, one heart aflame with love, beauty and inspiration can give faith to thousands. Seek out those that are brighter than yourself. Especially people who live in the mode of goodness. Gain their friendship and soon you will also be growing brighter. Be a light unto yourself and others. Association with good-hearted, faithful and inspiring people will make you brighter as well. You'll continually get brighter by associating with bright people.

YOUR ENVIRONMENT

Your immediate environment is another type of association that's vital to growth and abundance. What you surround yourself with on a daily basis is one of the most powerful determinates of your ability to grow and change. What is the predominating energy in your environment? Is it uplifting, inspiring? Mode of goodness? Passionate? Cheerful? Or is it dim, drab, limiting and depressing? Remember the energetic modes we discussed in Chapter Two? They are Illumination, Energy and Inertia. All the people, objects and environments that you surround yourself with, reflect the nature of these three modes and will have a corresponding effect upon your consciousness.

The Asian art of *Feng Shui* and its Indian counterpart called *Vastu* are systems of traditional knowledge that recognize the relationship of objects, environments and furniture in relation to personal psychology and prosperity. It's so important to keep your living space clean, bright and free of clutter. In other words, for optimum benefit, it's best to surround yourself with the mode of goodness, which is clean, natural, wholesome and open. It heralds greater growth and insight. Replace torn cushions and clothing. Involve yourself with upbeat, bright and enthusiastic people. Eat healthy foods and think positive and empowering thoughts. These are also forms of positive association, and they attract and build rapport with new and positive associations. Your inner and outer environments are a reflection of each other. Increase the quality in either and both will come up in quality.

RAPPORT WITH NATURE

One day when my children were still young, and the weather was warm and pleasant. My wife Sue and I, along with the kids, decided to enjoy a pleasant walk in the woods of Fall Creek. It was always a special treat to visit our favorite swimming hole there. There's an ancient pine tree fallen across the creek which creates a lovely little waterfall with a deep mysterious pool of very cold water. We loved to jump off the huge log into the swirling depths of that pool, always emerging feeling refreshed and renewed by the delightful natural experience of the brisk clean water. There's a certain timeless quality to be found in the simplicity of such moments and keeping up an active rapport with the natural environment has such a profoundly beneficial influence upon our consciousness. In his essays upon nature and beauty, Ralph Waldo Emerson wrote:

"Nature is the herald of inward and eternal beauty."

It was so inspiring to see my happy children playing and laughing in the scattered shafts of sunlight under the tangled roots of a creek side tree. The sight of my wife standing waist deep in that dark green emerald pool with her long wet hair fallen in delicate patterns over her shoulders and down her back was a vision of loveliness that evoked appreciation for the sacred feminine beauty reflected in all women. Her fair English features glowing white against the contrast of that enchanted emerald pool recreated the lovely image of a Celtic maiden bathing in a sacred well.

Whenever I visited that primeval redwood forest I found myself transported to a state of almost rapturous yet simple childlike appreciation. I think this was due to the conspicuous absence of the frantic passionate activity so characteristic of human society in this modern age, as well as the predominance of wholesome living energy that surrounded us in the forest. The forest is predominated by the energetic mode of growth and goodness. The *sattvic* quality that nourishes inner growth and appreciation. There's such an abundance of life in the forest. It always refreshes our inner being. I like to say that *"Nature is food for the soul."*

The deep forest never fails to impart a sense of sacredness and beauty that refreshes my spirit and renews my creativity. It reminds me of a passage from the *Dhamapada* that states: *"Holy is the forest, holy is the place where the senses are at peace."* Once while walking down the wooded path and appreciating the conscious living energy of the forest I began to feel the collective consciousness of the trees around me. Each tree has its own energy and expression and I believe each tree is an individual conscious living soul — a divine spark of the infinite all-pervading consciousness from which all objective material manifestations arise, by whom all are maintained and again dissolved in due course of time. This understanding of the paradigm of the conscious self awakens appreciation for all life forms, especially in the sacred tabernacle of nature.

As I walked further down the path I thought about how these souls all about me in tree forms have the same spiritual potentialities as I. However, due to their past desires and actions they have found their way to their current stationary forms. This of course is commonly known as the universal law of *karma*, or action and reaction. According to the concept of karmic law, as represented in the world's spiritual literatures, the eternal soul expresses its power of choice and reaps a corresponding circumstance and form. A more fully expressed consciousness is the great advantage of the human form of life, for it affords one the opportunity to question and seek out a more profound experience and abundant understanding of life, a chance to grow more deeply. As I continued my walk I began to consider what qualities might be gleaned from these tall friends quietly surrounding me. As I walked along I began to compose a poem that ran something like this:

silent sisters standing tall
wise in your silence
dumb to your years

stretch deep and high
eating water drinking air
wind wispering all

filtered light holy sight
to breathe what we leave
then leave what we need

ancient standing
rising young
patient forgiving

rough coated ladies
of sheltering green
blessed are these
the sheltering trees

HUMBLE AS THE GRASS

On my walks in the deep forest I would often think that if there is an infinite reality that underlies all existence, perhaps it may communicate a subtle wisdom to those who are patiently receptive and prayerful enough to listen. One way to develop such intuitive receptivity is to keenly observe the energetic rhythms of nature. An intimate rapport with nature brings forth a rich array of profound insights.

Perhaps by such receptivity one may begin to comprehend the spiritual subtlety that gives rise to manifest nature. When we say "nature," we must then ask, whose nature? When we observe a potency, like the whole of material nature, we can logically infer that there must be a potent source, like the sun and sunshine. The sun is the potent source. The shine is the potency. There must be many parables and metaphors of nature's wisdom in the varied cultures of the world. One that comes to mind is that of the fifteenth century mystic saint of West Bengal India, Sri Chaitanya Dev who once said; *"One who is humbler than a blade of grass, more tolerant than a tree, who gives due honor to others without desiring it for himself, is qualified to call upon the Holy names of God."*

This beautiful verse must be the expression of the deep devotional mood of a true saint. It is very profound in the way it utilizes the simple and universal elements of grass and trees to demonstrate a practical methodology for attaining unity with Divinity. By aligning oneself with the harmonious qualities of humility and tolerance one might possibly invite the descending grace of the divine underlying reality.

To be humbler than a blade of grass must imply an extreme flexibility in the face of an unpredictable Divine Providence. Unpredictable, because the divine reality as an Infinite spiritual personality, has free choice, volition and inconceivable mutually contradictory potencies with which to express itself. I suppose what I'm trying to say is that the Supreme Reality must by definition contain infinite potentiality and personality and is therefore never static, but on the contrary, dynamic and ever showing infinite color, movement and expression. As we in the human condition are endowed with an incredible range of thought and movement perhaps our potent spiritual source is similarly endowed.

Rapport with nature can grow your appreciation and gratitude for this amazing experience of life. Appreciating the gifts of nature can ignite an enduring faith in the heart of a person sincerely searching for a more deeply meaningful life. The humility of grass is a very nice metaphor for the type of flexibility that is an important quality in the life of those that would seek to understand life's deepest mysteries. For instance, if we rigidly maintain an inflexible and dogmatic idea of life, of Divinity, and the nature of reality, we unidimensionalize and limit our own experience of that reality, and thereby stunt our own potential for spiritual understanding and unfoldment.

Often the adversities we encounter in life offer us a valuable opportunity to connect with that which is really substantial in life. For when we suffer, we also question the nature of our existence. We naturally begin to pray and seek meaning from a higher or deeper source.

Practicing humility can place us in a vulnerable position. Which necessitates a deeper type of self-reliant faith. Faith is a profound trust in the unknown. It's a smile on the face of uncertainty, and it is, as the Native Americans would say *"a path with heart."*

Walking through this magnificent forest I was considering how flexibility and attentiveness could be helpful qualities in our search for meaningful abundance. Realization of higher truths often comes more easily in these precious moments amid nature's bounty. Souls such as ourselves, who are constantly preoccupied with the objects of our senses, are conditioned into a linear and mostly materialistically myopic view of life. Perhaps we could be shaken out of this conditioned stupor by the introduction of a broader perspective, a revelation or epiphany, a ray of understanding more accessible in these quiet moments. Perhaps like the seasons there are scheduled human epiphanies or cyclical revelations, like periodic light penetrating the cloud cover of human ignorance, illuminating our history, our lives, our hearts.

Along these lines of thought we can surmise the reason for theistic plurality or religious diversity in the world. A diversity of peoples, cultures and temperaments will necessitate a healthy plurality of approach towards the source. Genuine tolerance and flexibility can facilitate a broader understanding of this diversity and its value to the corresponding culture and circumstances in which it has arisen. Perhaps religious multiplicity is an expression of Divine compassion in order to compensate for the various gradations of conditioned consciousness found in human cultures. Whether it is the primitive theism of the animistic or shamanistic element worshiper, the natural harmony of Native Americans, Pagans and Taoists, the faith and devotion of Christianity or the sophisticated theology of the Upanishadic brahminical culture of India. All have a valid approach if there is sincerity in the heart.

The use of a tree as a metaphor for tolerance is also a very nice example used by Sri Chaitanya Dev. A tree remains silent even while the woodcutter chops away its branches. Moreover, it does not simply remain inactive but even gives shelter from the sun and perhaps even drops fruit that may be enjoyed by the aggressor. It brings to mind the example of how Christ blessed and forgave those that tortured and crucified him. Perhaps he was so absorbed in divine love of the Father that he was willing to *"Die to Live,"* as well as even bless those that hastened His demise. Like a *Boddhisattva,* he lived and died for the upliftment of others. By giving honor to others without requiring any honor in return we open ourselves to humiliation, and when we are downtrodden, humiliated and hurt, it becomes possible to genuinely cry out sincerely for divine grace, illumination and enlightenment.

It's easy to feign humility, but as Mother Teresa once said; *"To know real humility one must accept humiliation."* It seems that in this verse, Sri Chaitanya Dev offers us valuable advice how we may practice tolerance and humility as an integral tool to create the requisite vulnerability that leads to genuine wisdom that is born of sincere humility. It is a deep wisdom that leads to a state of abiding love towards all creatures and a natural harmony with the universal interest.

It would seem reasonable to conjecture that these characteristics of tolerance and humility open the heart, and when practiced sincerely, may foster the aspiration to abandon the false ego of mastership over the environment. Relinquishing our thirst for acquisition and exploitation and opening our lives to the possibility of living in a state of abundant spiritual grace. It's interesting how the wholesome natural atmosphere of the forest can calm the mind and bring about a favorable mood for the contemplation of life, death and the mysteries of consciousness. No doubt that is precisely why the saints, druids, mystics, yogis and sages of the past often resorted to the deep forests and remote hilltops as they have in India and Tibet for many millennium. Make peace with nature. She will nurture your soul.

TRANSPARENT LOVE

When my daughter was three we shared one of the simplest yet profound moments of our lives. It was the first time she consciously gave me a gift. We had a lovely garden at that time and were living in the Santa Cruz mountains. It was a beautiful day and we were in our garden when unexpectedly she picked up a small pebble and said: *"Daddy, I love you!"* As she placed it into my hand. It was the most touching and transparent act of spontaneous genuine love. On the bhakti yoga path we seek to express our hearts with this type of genuine clean love. It is selfless, it is without motive, and it is authentic. Such exchanges are transformative in their profound and simple beauty. They open our heart chakra and give us a glimpse of the type of profound love that human beings are capable of. There are five primary flavors of spiritual loving exchanges, and these are called rasa. What my daughter expressed was vatsalya rasa or love for the parent or guardian. We experience these relations everyday but rarely with the type of purity that is without personal motives.

As adults we can unlearn the self cherishing that covers our pure expression of love by adopting a devotional view towards ourselves, our lives, and our relationship with divinity. It's not a complicated affair but requires attention, sincerity and practice. Carl Jung met with some Hopi Elders in the 20's and they told him *"The whites think too much with their heads."* Puzzled, Jung inquired: How do you think? The chief then smiled and touched his heart. Attention to the interior life is the crown of a life well lived, and loved, and enriches all of our relationships.

CHAPTER FIVE
GENEROSITY

*"Real generosity toward the future lies in
giving all to the present."*
-Albert Camus

GIVE GENEROUSLY

How, what, and how much you give to life will to a large extent determine the quality of your life in many ways. Giving is getting in disguise. It's an investment. It's a deposit into your heart and the hearts of others. Paradoxically, by giving we are truly gaining. Every auspicious undertaking should begin with with a generous spirit of giving. Practicing generosity is the foundation of your personal contribution to life. Give your time, energy and most of all your affection and kindness to others. By doing so you contribute to a better quality of life for yourself and others. Generosity is active faith in the absolute abundance of the universe. It puts you in the zone of prosperity and abundance. It's one of the most powerful keys to your continued growth and abundance, but it must be an active living expression in the medium of your personal and business relationships. To take generous action activates abundance.

Action is an investment. Yes, all action is an investment, for in the circle of life your every contribution has its energetic return. The quality and quantity of energy sent forth determines the nature of the returning reaction. If there is a particular type of experience, especially recurring experience, happening in your life, you need not look much farther than your own mind for its origin. As you sow, so shall you reap. This is perennial wisdom but its also recognizable by modern science, and it's measurable.

EXPLOITATION OR DEDICATION

Most human interactions are governed by three principle modalities, and they are:

Exploitation

Renunciation

Dedication

When two people meet their interactions will be governed by these three modalities, which will determine the flavor of the experience. If I just want to sell you something with the sole purpose of getting something for myself, that's exploitation. People exploit other people for money, prestige, sex, fame, comfort, security and a host of other reasons, but the bottom line is selfishness. Few people are completely exploitive and most of us do exploit others to some degree, and there may be many valid reasons why we do so, such as fear, hope and desire. However, this is the lowest rung on the energetic ladder.

When desires are frustrated, when relations in romance or business don't work out or go sour we often run to the illusion of renunciation. This is an artificial state of attempting to hold the world at bay, of keeping ourselves aloof from human relations in order to avoid the hurt and disappointments that often accompany our experiences. The classic, "I'll never fall in love again," is not just a song title but the title of some people's mental states of withdrawal from meaningful interaction. It never lasts because no man or woman is an island and none of us can exist in this day and age without meaningful human interaction. We are truly *"one of another."* Dedication is the healthier of these modalities because it is aligned with the basic nature of the human spirit to give and the universal laws of harmony and symbiosis. This is unity in diversity. We are meant to uniquely give, to contribute and to share. This is where the fun is. This is where love is, and love, unity and affectionate exchange is what every human being is seeking in one way or another. And we dedicate ourselves in five primary ways:

As neutral associates

As servants

As friends

As guardians

As lovers

These are the five primary relations in which we can dedicate or contribute to the well being and benefit of others. In business relations we generally maintain a neutral emotional relationship, but within these dealings we can upgrade to service and friendly relations and even the guardian-like caring for the well being of others may be manifest, depending on the context and industry.

Find a way to dedicate your contribution for the well being and betterment of others, even if it's only a simple blessing upon a stranger. It may be small or large but if it's yours and if it's sincere, and from the heart, it will be of great value. Now, let's look at this thing called authenticity, your unique gift.

FIND YOUR AUTHENTICTY

Authenticity is a quality often overlooked or understated but certainly extolled in literature, film and media. You know, the simple genuine and honest James Stewart type character that often bumbles and mumbles his way through trials and tribulations set upon him by clever and conniving adversaries. Somehow the hero always comes out on top in the end because of his sincerity, and invariably the clever and smarter antagonist trips himself up with his own wicked plans. It's a scenario that's been used over and over again in books and films.

There's a saying: *"sincerity is invincible."* Authenticity is a form of natural sincerity of character. It can be expressed in many ways through love, art, music, literature, faith and even business. When you find your *"Path with a Heart"* you'll be a walking, talking example of authenticity. From this genuine state of sincerity you'll begin to understand how you can make your own unique contribution to the world. It may be small, it may be grand, but if it's sincere and genuine, it will be worthwhile. When we contribute to the well being of others, we grow. It's a win-win situation. As I stated earlier, giving is getting in disguise. Make a contribution to life and you'll always have enough. Your sincerity and authenticity will assist you in identifying the best way you can contribute to your friends, family and community.

The dictionary defines sincerity as the quality or condition of being authentic, trustworthy, or genuine. I like to think of authenticity as undisputed credibility. It's the totality of a persons' character speaking to you. There's a saying, "people don't care how much you know until they know how much you care." That's an example of authenticity. It's who they are that really counts. Not what they can do or say.

Authenticity is your total power of character in motion. In martial arts a person is trained to use their whole body in such a way that the total organism becomes a unified power. People who are untrained in martial arts will often fight the old school way with only their arms, but someone who can move their whole body congruently and fluidly as in a dance will be infinitely more effective. Their body becomes one big unified coiled spring of powerful muscle-groups congruently effective in their unified and flowing motion.

Finding authenticity is related to our inner calling or intrinsic nature that expresses our unique dharma. It's the area of your greatest strength and ability. Authenticity is your total being speaking to the environment and this becomes a truly powerful expression when the individual has unified all aspects of the personality and physiology in congruency and elegance. Jerry Garcia had great musical congruency that touched the hearts of many. His music was also very honest and authentic. Picasso was authentic in his originality. Maxfield Parrish was unique in his authentic creativity of style. Carlos Santana has great musical panache; this is another form of authenticity as well as a great contribution to our musical enjoyment. Mother Teresa had great authenticity in her sincerity and compassion. Martin Luther King had a sincere faith and desire to free others from suffering and oppression. Einstein had his unique brilliance, and Buddha had his unique clarity.

Clarity and unified emotional and psychological energy consciously directed generate great personal power. Most of us fail to achieve greater results in our lives because our minds and emotions are splayed-out all over the place. Think of the example of rope. One thin thread of fiber is not very strong, but unite it with many others and its strength is greatly magnified. Your unified mind and emotions are a powerful force. Back it with sincerity and authenticity and you've got an amazing recipe for success, no matter what you choose to do with it.

For most of us, returning to our natural, unified state of authentic congruency requires first and foremost a return to simplicity, for simplicity brings clarity. For example, if you wish to retrieve something valuable from the bottom of a pool and the surface is ruffled with ripples and disturbance you will be unable to see down to the depths where your object lies. But if you practice patience and self-control, allowing the water to calm down, you will see deeply and clearly and then dive directly to the treasure.

STAND UP TO YOURSELF

Another important point is to challenge your old programming that may be unconsciously limiting your results without your conscious knowledge. You see, most of us absorbed our core beliefs and ideas about what's possible from the attitudes, beliefs and actions of our parents and siblings in our early formative years. Not only that but we learned "how' to think and respond emotionally. We learned patterns of thinking and emotional response.

Many of these modalities of thought lay below our conscious awareness where they undermine our efforts like roving thieves in the night. Our task is to bring them to the conscious light of day, for in doing so we diminish their hold upon us and they vanish like mist before the rising sun.

If our parents constantly fretted over a fearful future or were often worried about having enough money to pay the bills we were living in the penumbra of that emotional environment. Although as teenagers we often questioned our parents' beliefs, values and emotional responses, we certainly were immersed in their energies and absorbed much of their behavior unconsciously.

It's important to look at this residual material within our own inner environment and sort out the supportive from the destructive. As I mentioned previously, we have emotional and genetic set-points that are our own natural energetic levels, which are further embellished upon by our experiences and as we grow from children to teenagers to young adults we develop patterns of behavior and thinking that may or may not serve our better interests in life.

The combination of these behavioral patterns and habitual ways of thinking as well as our unconscious beliefs may sometimes obscure from our own vision the realization of our own inner strengths, abilities, potentiality and subsequent authenticity. So I encourage you to get clear about what you're carrying around in your inner environment, write it down, sort it out and discard any limiting patterns by over-writing them with more realistic and empowering beliefs. Recording and examining your dreams can be very effective in uncovering unconscious material and raising them to the light of conscious awareness.

DREAMS AND THEIR POWER

Receptivity, openness, and flexibility of thought are also effective aids to creativity and the ability to identify your unique contribution. To dogmatically hold to one limited view of experience forecloses human creative potential by an irrational obsession with only one kind of meaning. Experiences take on the meanings we impart to them. Besides uncovering unconscious material that we may have repressed, examining dreams is a great way to develop greater flexibility of mind.

Every night the creative door swings wide open as we enter the unlimited potentiality of the dream state. For thousands of years, long before recorded history, shamans and indigenous cultures throughout the world have worked with dreams to gain greater insight and find guidance, direction and power. In particular, Dr. Patricia Garfield mentioned in her book, Creative Dreaming, that the Senoi tribe of Malaysia developed their amazing culture around dream work and as a result, they had a very healthy and happy psychology and a low incidence of violence.

Scientific research over the past several decades has clearly shown that not only do all humans dream, but all mammals dream. Studies in sleep patterns have clearly demonstrated REM patterns and corresponding dream states to be a universal phenomena among mammals and marsupials. Those whom claim to not dream are in reality simply unskilled in their ability to recall their dreams.

Research is now revealing that all living beings participate in the dream state. Even plants have cyclical metabolic patterns analogous to dormant patterns of rest. Dreaming is woven into the very fabric of our biology and may be argued to be a key element in our evolutionary growth as conscious individuals. What power we have for self-transformation in our dreams! Virtually anything is possible. In dreams we can permit ourselves the impossible, and experience it.

The dream researchers of the past ten decades have left us an enormous body of literature filled with many clues to help sort the symbolism and archetypal imagery of dreams. Though the discoveries of these inner pioneers by no means wholly define these experiences, their past contributions can help speed us on our way in gaining a deeper living relationship with our own unconsciousness and the dream material that emerges every night. It's remarkable how much we can learn about ourselves through the simple procedure of recording and examining our dreams. Dreaming is essentially a way that we communicate with ourselves.

Freud researched sexual interpretations. Alder examined the struggle for meaning. Jung sought to understand universal archetypes and Edgar Cayce revealed that much of our subconscious material may be utilized for healing the physical and emotional body. Mary Forster was a nineteenth century pioneer of lucid dreaming and her great contribution laid the groundwork for much of the current work being done in this field. Especially, the practice of incubating lucid awareness and flying in dreams.

For me personally, the great and exciting prospect that dream research reveals is the immense fluidity of consciousness.

There is a remarkable flexibility of ability, creativity and personal power inherent in dreams, and as one becomes more acquainted with one's own consciousness, remarkable abilities manifest. Dream study can facilitate a valuable carry-over benefit of understanding into our waking lives. Such skillfulness in managing internal states can lead to immense joy and freedom by liberating us from the binding and burdening effects of habitual thought patterns.

Nobel prize wining scientist Niels Bohr dreamed of a pleasant day at the races and realized that the marked lanes of the race track were analogous to the fixed orbits that electrons are required to follow in their circulation around atomic nuclei. Albert Einstien realized the Theory of Relativity after a dream he had in adolescence in which he rode a sled past the speed of light. The periodic Table of Elements was dreamed by Mendelejeff in the shape of chamber music.

Most fascinating is the story of how a dream inspired the invention of the sewing machine, which liberated clothing manufacture from its pre-industrial medieval form into the modern technological industrial force that has revolutionized our social, economic and political experience. It literally released the floodgates of the Industrial Revolution.

It happened like this...

In 1844 Elias Howe was frustrated and exhausted in his continued effort to invent the modern sewing machine. Falling asleep at his workbench he had a dream or rather a nightmare, in which he was chased by cannibalistic African aboriginals who subsequently captured him and placed him in a pot of boiling water. The boiling water loosened his bonds and as he repeatedly attempted to climb out of the pot, the natives poked him with their spears, which he noticed had holes in the spear tips. When he awoke he was in a disturbed state, however the memory of the spear points with holes in the tips caused him to realize that if he threaded the needle at the tip instead of the blunt end, his sewing machine would be far more efficient. Remarkably, his dream directly resulted in the modern sewing machine. Perhaps you've experienced your own amazing insights through dreams?

Dreams are a great source of creativity and are a great ally in understanding ourselves. They speak a universal language of symbol and metaphor and when observed over a lifetime may reveal many hidden elements of our present biology, psychology and personal conscious evolution.

When we lose conscious awareness and fall asleep, or fall into unconsciousness, there is a period of un-awareness until dream images begin to arise. Some of these images are based upon our daily experiences and may be considered immediate karmic traces, or *"day-residue,"* which percolate into jumbled dream sequences of a pleasing or unpleasant nature. There is another class of impressions that have been classified as coming from previous existences as well, and may remain as subtle karmic traces that only arise when secondary causes become favorable. The secondary causes for their appearance can be stimulated either in dream or in waking states. Both the dreaming and waking states of consciousness are ultimately influenced by the karmic obscurations, subtle occlusions and misidentified conceptualizations.

The practice of present moment awareness in the day can sometimes be carried over into this dream state enabling one to experience lucidity within the dream. In effect you wake up within the dream and realize that... "I am dreaming." This experience is often accompanied by a great exhilaration for its accompanying realization of almost infinite possibility heightens one's experience of states and dream activities that transcend what is normally possible in our daily experience. It is possible at this point to begin manifesting conscious control of dreams.

One can fly in the sky, manifest a light body, travel to distant places, transform fire into water, and manifest celestial environments, forests and fields of magnificent beauty. In effect, experience all the wonders of unbridled conscious imagination, for according to Tibetan Dream Yoga, our awareness is as much as seven times enhanced in dream states.

In reality, our nature is of subtle conscious existence and one can sometimes more efficiently perform spiritual practice in dreams unencumbered by physical limitations. For the subtle realm is closer to reality than are the grosser material manifestations of our waking hours.

Beyond this ability however, is the greater possibility to realize the transient nature of all phenomena and to carry this awareness and its transformative power back over into the waking hours of our daily life. Accompanying this is the further realization of the fluidity of consciousness and the realization that our only limitations are those that we impose upon ourselves through attachment, aversion, fear and ignorance. Dreams can help us to realize the unlimited potentiality of our intrinsic conscious nature.

All of our experiences, of both psychological and emotional states have their origins within our own consciousness, for we are indeed the authors of our own experience. Dreams are populated by the personifications of our own inner processes and by acquainting ourselves with these processes we gain greater self-unification and mastery. Which in turn leads to a more enriched and satisfying experience of life. Through awareness, knowledge and detachment one gains greater facility for conscious control in both dream and waking states, as well as the ability to manifest every experience of life as a positively transformative spiritual experience of growth and realization. Daily practice is necessary and is rewarded almost immediately, for as we internally change, so does the experience of our external life. The rewards are great for those who inquire within. Inner liberty is true freedom, and generosity is one of the foundations of a free mind and heart.

DARE TO BE YOU

Its far more empowering to tell yourself that you are a conscious being of infinite possibility, meant for growth and expansion, than to limitedly define yourself in a fixed state, fixed in attitudes, stuck in behavior, and limited to one view or way of expression. Life is a dynamic growing and expanding process. Energies that are alive and healthy are in motion. Energies that are static are decaying and preparing to be recycled for a future phase of growth and living dynamic expansion.

Be generous with yourself and dare to live, be independent in your thought and behavior. Generosity is also a type of flexibility. Don't be afraid to call the bluff on some of your old negative and limiting attitudes. Be adventurous, think for yourself and don't go along with the herd mentality of *"business as usual."* You are unique. You are beautiful, and you have your own unique and special contribution to make in life. Giving is getting in disguise; make a contribution to life and you'll always have enough. Abundant flow is cyclical. Invest in abundance by giving to yourself and others without motivation of return. Give as an act of returning to the healthy flow.

Believe in your own uniqueness and creativity. Challenge the various assumptions that were unconsciously adopted in your early years. Make new plans, new choices, and find new friends and associates that help you to grow and expand into the person you want and believe you can be. Your own authentic expression of self is the greatest and most sincere gift you can give to the world and everyone around you. It is your own personal expression of living dynamic absolute abundance.

THE DHARMA OF GIVING

Why do acts of kindness, generosity and service seem so natural? Why are those unique individuals in our culture who heroically sacrifice themselves for the betterment of others lauded, extolled and commemorated? Persons such as Mother Teresa, Martin Luther King, Gandhi, Srila Prabhupad, Jesus, and the Buddha.

It's because giving is our essential nature, and everyone knows this deeply, often unconsciously. The essence of our being is to grow and love. It is synonymous with our essential conscious self. Love could be termed as the "food" of our soul. Love is most purely demonstrated by self-giving without expectation of return.

The idea is to unselfishly satisfy others with the sole ideal of their well being and happiness. Isn't this what we naturally do when we love someone? This is the ideal of devotion and dedication, and because everything in the universe operates on the principle of karma or "action and reaction," return of love to the giver is guaranteed, which is a beautiful way to free ourselves from giving with the secret motive of selfishly getting something back. Abundance and sharing is the nature of the circle of life.

One of my favorite forms of generosity is to share music with children. Over the last decade, my wife and I have been invited to share Indian music with grade school classes. This is so fun and uplifting. I bring along a sitar, harmonium, drums and tampura. The children love seeing, hearing, and touching these exotic instruments. I like to demonstrate them with Indian devotional folk songs and chants. It's one of the most rewarding ways I've found to generously share something uplifting with others. Every investment in the heart and wisdom of others is an investment in our own present and future goodness.

CIRCLES

Ralph Waldo Emerson wrote in his essay entitled Circles:

"The eye is the first circle; the horizon which it forms is the second; and throughout nature this primary figure is repeated without end."

Everywhere in nature we find a cyclical flow. Abundance is the understanding of this flow and the word "affluence" literally means, "to flow." When we give abundantly from the heart we clear our hearts to receive more abundantly. And so the flow continues on in a cyclic way. Everything moves in a circle...day and night, the seasons, the planets, the cycles of life and death... circles. The Beatles once sang: "and in the end, the love you take, is equal to the love you make." Circles...flow...giving and receiving. Abundance, whether it be, material wealth, natural resources or emotional/spiritual love, is a continuum of flow, a dynamic state of favorable flux, an exciting dancing ebb and flow of energies. When our hearts are open, the channels of abundant flow are open in our lives. We are free to abundantly give and receive. Flexibility and faith assist our understanding of these fundamental truths.

PRACTICE YOUR HAND TO GIVE

Personally, I find that if I'm coming up short monetarily or emotionally it means I have a deficit somewhere. My own lack of giving spirit has constricted the flow. It's time to "prime the pump" and restore the flow. There's a saying in India, "Practice your hand to give," meaning that if I have nothing of vlaue to give then I can at least give a handful of dirt or ash. The point is to restore the mood of giving, which is a way to restore the flow of abundant currency, regardless of the specific energy involved. Taking my place in this beautiful dance of life with the spirit of giving, I need not concern myself about the when and where of "my" turn. Love, abundance and opportunity will come to me, just as surely as the sun will rise.

When we truly love another, the incidentals of life do not interrupt love's continuity. Nor are there conditions attached. Clean love has no selfish desire. You do not love because you want something, but because it is the very nature of the inner self to love, and the symptom of that love is a willingness to give. This restores us to our powerful and natural dharmic state from which we can make our greatest contribution to the well-being of others.

When our love is realized in service to all beings it harmonizes all action to the plane of higher Reality. When it is perfected in service to that Reality, it rains down a shower of auspiciousness that floods the heart with joy. Love is an autocrat, love is where we're at, when we give up our disguise. Giving and contributing to the welfare of others is the best way to abundantly express our inner nature of love. Be a selfless giver... paradoxically, its the greatest gain.

CONTRIBUTE WISELY

As I mentioned at the outset of this chapter, action is an investment. For in the circle of life your every contribution has it's energetic return. This of course is what the ancients called Karma, and what we call cause and effect. The quality and quantity of energy sent forth determines the nature of the returning reaction. If there is a particular type of experience, especially recurring experience, happening in your life, you need not look much farther than your own mind for it's source. As you sow, so shall you reap.

If you're like most people, you will trade your precious daily hours for a paycheck. Hopefully, it's doing something you love, or at least something you like, or something that contributes to a cause, product or service that benefits others. I'm totally grateful that I have, for the most part, been self-employed for most of my adult life. It's not because I'm smart or clever or had all the good breaks. It's really because as a child, I identified my primary interest in arts and as I grew I was fortunate to be able to apply and grow in these abilities in practical ways. When you think about it, the common stereotype of the artist is of the impoverished or "starving artist." Fortunately, I was able to bypass this mindset by becoming involved in business-related graphic design, advertising and ultimately, commercial sign-making. There's a joke among musicians that reflects the "starving artist" mentality.

Question: What do you call a musician without a girlfriend? Answer: Homeless!

Well, I'm no great artist but I am truly grateful to have found my passion, my forte, my raison díetra, and to have been fortunate enough to recognize the opportunities that allowed me to apply my talents in a useful way so that they grew into marketable skills like graphic design, illustration, book production and sign manufacturing. You see, I'm in a service industry. Sign making provides an important, even vital service to business and the economy. Businesses need signs when they are going into business, when they are maintaining and promoting business, as well as when they are going out of business! Graphic design, printing and sign making are the communication side of business, and businesses, especially small to mid-size business need these vital communication services to attract, maintain and service their clientele. There's a saying, "A business without a sign, is a sign of no business." Of course these days a website is also essential and over the past ten years my business has become increasingly internet-driven. It's the most efficient way to do business and benefits the environment by cutting down on automobile emissions, toxic fax paper, and a host of other unnecessary activities and collateral materials.

The point I'm driving at is that contributing and giving are essential, but do it wisely. How you communicate greatly effects how you are perceived by others. In other words, the quality of your communication is the quality of your business, your relationships and your life.

There's a difference in working for the betterment of others and directly working for them. Now, you will rarely become more abundant by working for someone else. It's a practical consideration, worth deep consideration. Because if you trade the precious moments of your day punching someone else's clock, you'll be contributing to someone else's prosperity and dreams and shelving your own. That's fine if your personal vision is supported by the work or contributes to the greater good of society, but all the while your own clock will be ticking away your own valuable time in the background as your personal dreams fade into the mist. Besides, as a successful entrepreneur, you will be in a better position of personal freedom and economic abundance to make more significant contributions for the greater welfare of others.

As a young man I first worked in an antique shop when I was twelve, then as a salesman, then as a handyman, and a film lab technician until I arrived at what I really wanted to do at the time, which was illustration and design. Often in our late teens and twenties we migrate through several positions until our professional life path begins to unfold and we clearly identify our strengths. There's nothing wrong with working for others who are proficient or successful in our area of interest. This can be quite helpful as a preparatory phase before we launch our own projects. In fact, this can be a very useful and educational link in growing our talents. We will gain great strength, insight and momentum by associating with those who are already successful in the direction we also wish to go.

BECOME AN ENTREPRENEUR

You will also have far more to contribute to other people and society at large if you have the professional freedom that self-employment and an entrepreneurial lifestyle allow. Let's look at this unusual word entrepreneurial.

It's a noun from the old French, from the word *entreprendre,* meaning to undertake. The literal definition from Webster's Dictionary is: one who organizes, manages, and assumes the risks of a business or venture. My own definition runs something like this: to assume risk, to be intrepid.

The etymology of intrepid, comes from the Latin, intrepidus, trepidus means alarmed. An intrepid state of mind is characterized by resolute fearlessness, fortitude, and endurance, as in an intrepid explorer. The second half of the word would seem to imply strong nerves. Neurial, as in entrepre-neurial. Of, relating to, or affecting a nerve or the nervous system.

An entrepreneur is a person who has an abundant sense of possibility and recognizes opportunities. He or she will be willing to assume significant accountability for the inherent risks and the outcome because they know that there is a greater reward and 100% return when you invest in yourself and your own growth, skills and abilities. Here are a few more facts that should encourage you to find a way to work for yourself, and make your own unique contribution.

Consider these facts:

• Entrepreneurs embrace a level of personal, professional or financial risk to pursue opportunity because they know the benefits far outweigh the risks. In other words, they see opportunity and value not cost or loss. Remember the old adage: "is the glass half full or half empty?"

• Entrepreneurs tend to identify a market opportunity and benefit themselves and others by organizing their resources effectively to accomplish an outcome that changes existing interactions within a given sector. Through the organization and application of their personal power they make contributions that transform themselves and the environment. Remember the story of Steve Jobs and the development of Apple Computers? Or Bill Gates and Microsoft?

• Business entrepreneurs are viewed as fundamentally important in the capitalistic society. Entrepreneurs are the pioneers and leaders in every field. Every new innovation from the stone tool to the personal computer is the result of the entrepreneurial spirit of exploration and implementation.

• Entrepreneurship, particularly among women in developing countries, seems to offer an improvement in the standard of living as well as a path out of poverty.

• Entrepreneurship is now growing at nearly three times the rate among women as it is among men. Social entrepreneurs act within a market aiming to create social value through the improvement of goods and services offered to the community. Their main aim is to offer a better service improving the community, as a whole and are often run as non-profit schemes.

An entrepreneurial mindset can be described as a group of personal dispositions, also known as entrepreneurial spirit, which lead to the innovative practice of identifying and or creating opportunities, then acting to manifest those opportunities in a productive way. This is absolute abundance in action. By utilizing the three keys mentioned in chapter three — Awareness, Assessment and Action — we exercise the entrepreneurial spirit and being an entrepreneur is one of the best ways to make a significant contribution to society.

Not everyone will feel they have the ability or skill to go into business for themselves, but I assure you that you have your own unique talent and abilities that can be developed in some way to contribute to the benefit of others. We all do. Identify them and begin sharing them and as you do so, those abilities will grow and manifest new opportunities, opportunities that present themselves for continued growth and further opportunities. One thing leads to another and once you've primed the pump, and established a flow you'll be surprised what comes your way. Get in the abundant flow of giving and contributing and these abilities will abundantly grow.

Remember, your future biological, economic, emotional and educational states are determined by your present thinking and actions, because your over-all life experience is always a product of your own consciousness. Contributing to the well being of others will help to consciously direct your life in a more abundant flow and lead you toward more refined and elegant states of existence. If you have more independence you will have more time and energy to give. Your contribution quotient will rise. More energy means more energy to contribute. More contribution means more opportunity to contribute, and more energy to do it with.

QUALITIES OF ENERGY

Speaking of energy, the general rule is this: The subtler, the lighter, the brighter, the better. Bright deeds of dharmic love, selfless service and harmony cause consciousness to brighten and rise to subtler expressions. Deeds of selfishness and harm are the cause of grosser, less aware, or constricted consciousness, the opposite of abundance. By harming others we create obstacles for ourselves. Remember, *"affection is the connection."*

Self-awareness and active contribution enables one to realize that each action is an investment in a future return either of a conscious abundant and liberating nature or a binding constricting effect. We make the choices, we experience the effects. We live in a cause and effect universe.

Choose wisely my friend. You are the architect of your own experiences. If you'd like to see more abundance all around you, begin by spreading it around yourself. Enter the energetic flow of abundance. Give generously of your time, energy and resources and you will see it all return in due course. Abundance is cyclical flow. And the best way to experience it is to join the dance of life by giving.

COMMUNITY

Community is something sacred. It is an expression of honoring the parts as they contribute to the whole. You can open your doors to more abundant energetic flow and celebrate your human unity through the social affection of community. This is a great way to increase the flow in your life and connect with others in a spirit of giving. This is one of the primary reasons I love living in a small town like Eugene, Oregon. It's quite pleasant to have daily encounters with friends and friends of friends who are all connected through the local community and activities of education, music, festivals and worship. It's enriching for everyone to have more personal interactions with other human beings.

There is a great mood of community and caring for other people and the environment here. And that affection for others has a tendency to grow beyond the borders of our small town into an appreciation for the plight of others in less abundant circumstances, like India or Haiti. As a spiritual expression, the affection in our hearts can grow beyond the limits of race and compassionately embrace other species as well, and indeed all life forms on this planet. Unity in diversity is recognition of the intrinsic value in all life forms. It grows by suspending the critical judgment of the culture, lifestyle or orientation of others.

Look to the core of the heart of life and you will find a universal desire for pleasure and the avoidance of pain. Look even deeper and you find love. Seek for this deep abiding spiritual love that unites all living beings in the beautiful energetic dance of life. Even the search will bring immense benefits.

Celebrate the diversity of life by being generous with your affection. Be grateful and honor others. In doing so you impart value to everything and everyone that surrounds you. Then, every street you walk will be an isle in the greater church of life. In the beautiful eyes of others you will see the beautiful love of God, the Source or Divinity as you conceive of it.

Your words will become nectar and your steps a dance of joy.
Each child will be your beloved son or daughter.
Every bird and animal your friend.
Each flower a growing smile.
Each moment sacred.
Each breath a prayer.
Holy presence.
You are.
Now.

Practicing generosity is the foundation of your personal contribution to life. Give your time, energy and most of all your affection and kindness to others. By doing so you contribute to a better quality of life for yourself and others. Sometimes I like to take my second hand inspirational books that I've read and insert a $5 dollar bill between the pages. I keep a few of these in my car and when I see one of those persons on the corner with a cardboard sign I offer it to them with love and the words; "Here is some wealth and wisdom, brother." It's a wonderful way to practice our hand to give as well as share some inspirational wisdom with someone who needs both.

Remarkably, you will glimpse the goodness in the nature of that person and find a similar growing goodness in yourself. Give freely, generously and with love. The very process itself is so uplifting for you the giver as well as your blessed recipient. Consider these thoughts:

Generosity is the best protection against poverty.
Compassion is the best protection against violence.
Awareness is the best protection against suffering.
Loving-kindness is the best protection against hatred.

Generosity is active faith in the absolute abundance of the universe. It puts you in the zone of prosperity and abundance. It's one of the most powerful keys to your continued growth and abundance.

Now let's explore the immense power of gratitude.

CHAPTER SIX
GRATITUDE, GRACE & GOODNESS

"Gratitude unlocks the fullness of life. It turns what we have into enough, and more. It turns denial into acceptance, chaos to order, confusion into clarity. It can turn a meal into a feast, a house into a home, a stranger into a friend. Gratitude makes sense of our past, brings peace for today, and creates a vision for tomorrow."

-Melody Beattie

As I mentioned in Chapter One, success means the ability to appreciate life for what it is at present. Success is a form of gratitude. Appreciation and gratitude are remarkable allies on the way to cultivating a self-contented mind, which is itself a great inner wealth. It is what we seek internally when we seek wealth externally. No one really cares about printed notes of paper and ink. It's the promise of inner freedom that money can supposedly buy us that is attractive. We mistakenly think material wealth will grant us peace from the struggles of life. However, studies have shown that material wealth actually complicates our lives.

It is from the platform of gratitude that we can begin to mentally construct our own personal vision of outer abundance, peace, and inner liberty. Applying gratitude to the daily experiences of our lives, conditions us for present moment satisfaction, which improves our relationship with ourselves, and others. Equally important is the idea that it also prepares us for greater future satisfaction as well. Life is more beautiful, powerful and meaningful when we pay attention to it in the present moment. We are in effect retraining ourselves to see value in everything and everyone, even the people and circumstances that annoy us.

I'll say this many times, abundance is a state of mind. Monetary abundance is only a symptom of that state. Satisfying and fulfilling relationships are the true wealth and delicious fruit of this abundant mentality. Make gratitude your starting point and you will have a strong foundation.

YOUR ENERGETIC BASE CAMP

Over and over again I'm going to remind you that energetic flow is the key to success in all areas of life. Abundance consciousness is a consciousness of this living flow. Now, all of us have something unconsciously operating in our lives called the pleasure/pain principle.

What we associate with pleasure we tend to move towards and what we associate with pain we tend to move away from. This often, unconscious process determines our subtle energetic base.

Are you moving towards a more fulfilling dream or are you running scared from a painful past or present? It makes a difference which direction you're going internally because if you're operating from a sense of lack you're feeding your unconscious mind a goal of continued lack. What is your energetic base? From what central idea does your life proceed? You need to identify this energetic base camp and make sure its aligned with an unshakable conviction of abundance, growth and possibility. If you center yourself in the wisdom of the self and approach every experience with gratitude, you will see a dramatic increase in the flow. Lets face it. Neither you, me or anyone else on this planet will ever be any happier by simply getting more stuff. Why? Because, the desire to get more stuff is an endless loop of cyclical desire. As soon as you get more, you want more. The thirst for "more" grows more and more, and desire is the shadow of a consciousness predominated by a sense of lack. Unbridled desire is poverty consciousness dressed up as achievement. Gratitude is the antidote. Gratitude is the watering of abundance. Its giving thanks before receiving, which is another form of faith. Faith in abundance, in goodness, and trust that what you need will show up when you need it.

The real secret to happiness is not getting what you want but wanting what you get, and a more refined version of this concept is to be grateful for everything that has already come. Try to grow a thirst for gratitude in all areas of your thinking, feeling and willing.

GRATITUDE HEALS ALL WOUNDS

Gratitude is also a very powerful ally in releasing negative attitudes. It's nearly impossible to be grateful and at the same time feel angry, resentful or hurt. We have much to be grateful for in life. If we think about it carefully, everything and everyone is a gift worthy of our gratitude.

The air we breathe, the water we drink, the food grains we eat, the sunlight, the rain and clouds. Our natural intuitive intelligence, and our physical bodies, the senses, the mind. All of our talents and abilities. These are but a few of the natural gifts that grace our lives by the presence of a higher power. An all-pervading intelligent power acknowledged by us as "Nature," the "Absolute," or "Godhead." If we count up our talents and personal abilities we will also have to acknowledge that these too are gifts worthy of our gratitude. For most talent is the combination of our interests and our efforts, fueled by the inspiration of a friend, family member, teacher or someone that inspired us in some way. We are all connected in the circle of life.

It's not an exaggeration to say that literally everything we have, and are, has been given to us, by others in some way. Our mothers and fathers gave us our physical bodies and genetic tendencies. Our education and intelligence was fostered and in a way, gifted to us by our teachers and professors. Our physical strength is given by the plants and grains we eat. Artists have given us beauty. Mystics, philosophers and clergy have inspired our faith. Great thinkers and innovators of the past have left records of their discoveries, which benefit us today. Employees create wealth for employers. Employers create opportunities for employees. Audiences benefit performers and repetition gives us ability. Gratitude for all of this is another form of affection, and affection is connection, positive connection. The kind of connection that communicates ability, insight and abundance from one life to another.

Often what comes to us comes through the channel of affection. Ultimately we are benefited by the affection and kindness of others. Through this channel we gain much nourishment, though we are often benefited through the "left-handed" channel of adversity as well.

If we make gratitude a daily practice and a prominent feature of our consciousness we will witness a dramatic transformation in our lives. If we learn to be grateful before we receive the gift we will witness greater abundance growing daily in our lives. To give thanks is to grow more prosperous internally and to outwardly live more joyfully. When this inner joy is practiced consistently and sincerely outer manifestations of prosperity are sure to follow. Abundant consciousness manifests abundant environments. Think about it. You have this ability right now.

If we look for goodness, we will find it everywhere, and come to see that every wave is favorable. It's all about how you frame your experiences and that's ultimately up to you. You have that power within you. This is your moment of power. Decide that all of your experiences have positive outcomes because they are lessons for you to grow in greater wisdom.

YOU FIND WHAT YOU ARE

Once there was a wise man sitting on a hillside. As he sat there enjoying the view above the town the sweet spring breeze blew upon him. The sun was shining brightly in a clear blue sky. The pleasant call of birds could be heard from all directions and he felt a deep contentment within himself.

After some time a young man approached grumbling and frowning and kicking a stone. He called out to the wise man, "Old man, what kind of people live in that town below?"

To which the wise man replied, "What kind of people did you meet in the last town?"

"They were mean and rotten," replied the young man. "I got outta there as soon as I could."

The wise man just nodded.

Then after some time, along came another man whistling and smiling. He called out to the wise man, "Excuse me sir, what manner of people live in that town below?"

The wise man replied, "What manner of men did you meet in the last place you visited. To which the man replied, "Oh they were all so very kind. It was hard to leave but I didn't want them to feel I was taking advantage of their generosity."

To which the wise man replied, "You'll find more people like that down below." You see, we attract to ourselves that which reflects our own nature. With clarity and gratitude we can gain the insight that our experience of life is subjective. Adversity can be transformed to our advantage when we ask *"What can I learn from this experience, how can I grow?"*

There was a queen in ancient times named Kunti Devi who actually prayed for adversity because she knew and acknowledged the transformative power of challenging experiences when they are re-framed as opportunities for growth and learning. We may not be that bold, but we can certainly examine the way we view our experiences and responses and transform each new experience, even negative and challenging ones, into opportunities for abundant growth by recognizing that its not a punishment but a lesson in the bigger school of energetic life. It's part of the flow, and flow is good. Flow is abundance.

Gratitude is the key to this deeper understanding.

Here's an experience I had that brought me greater appreciation and gratitude for all the abundance in my own life.

FROM DISASTER TO DELIGHT

It all began in 1998 when as you may recall, I described in Chapter Two how our family had been visiting my wife's parents in England and upon our return, circumstances brought about a move from living in a beautiful three bedroom house in the woods with gardens and acreage to a 4-man tent pitched on a hillside in Soquel. It was a humbling yet profoundly empowering experience because I realized that happiness was not so much related to what I "owned" but what I generated and carried within myself. I had reframed the big change from disaster to delight. We had scaled down all of our possessions from a three bedroom house to a one, ten foot by ten foot storage unit...and boy was that exhilarating!

I felt so free, so light, so liberated of the burden of possessing so much stuff. When you let go of a large accumulation of possessions, you feel an amazing lightness of being because whatever we "own" or possess keeps us unconsciously tethered. Releasing the attachment of ownership releases our consciousness and frees up emotional space as well. Just like when you dump a lot of extra files from your computer you immediately see a dramatic increase in your computers performance and speed.

Once I had all the things I wanted to keep stowed away nicely in my $50.00 a month storage unit, we began living a very simple lifestyle on the beautiful shady hillside in Soquel. It was a thirty-acre property that had become the ashram property of our local spiritual community and many of our friends lived in the several buildings or motor homes on the property. Our situation was a most simple affair. We erected a large four-man tent upon a small wooden deck constructed of pallets. Our living room, kitchen and dining area was a lovely shaded spot under a big oak tree!

We had a good deal of privacy as we were situated up a hillside with bushes all around the perimeter that gave a very nice private and natural feel to the location. We cooked on a propane gas stove and hiked down the hill to the showers or took bucket baths up on the hill. Because we had spent time in India we were already accustomed to these minor austerities and actually found them to be quite enjoyable in their natural simplicity, for our spiritual path had always held high the ideal of "*simple living and high thinking.*"

Most of the time the weather was warm and sunny and we felt like we were on an extended camping trip. It was fun, exhilarating and delightful as many of our friends who shared the property would stop by for tea under the trees and many of our meals were taken in the open air. There was also a large communal kitchen down the hill with an adjacent hall at the main building, which housed the ashram's central shrine.

All would rise at 4:30 am to attend morning services, sing the holy songs, and recite prayers. It was a beautiful and sacred experience to be in the company of so many kind and sincere spiritual seekers who were dedicating their lives to devotional practice. They were individuals of all ages and backgrounds who were all genuinely focused on the principles of *"simple living and high thinking."* There was a spirit of dedication and self-giving that permeated the property and all who lived there were enthusiastic to live a clean and uplifting yogic lifestyle. Fortunately there was also a large barn on the property with plenty of space where I was allowed to set up my sign workshop, and continue my business of sign manufacturing uninterruptedly.

Our children benefited immensely from this experience as well because they interacted with so many high-thinking and genuinely good people, several of whom were monks who had taken life-long vows of celibacy and spiritual purity. There was also the added benefit of a large group of children with whom our kids could play with throughout the enchanting and beautiful thirty acres.

We had a glorious summer on that hill and our teacher from India came to visit, which brought many more disciples, friends and seekers from all over the world to the property and lent an ever increasing and uplifting festive energy to the whole experience. It increased our deep gratitude for the simpler yet more deeply important aspects of life, such as spiritual focus and growth, like-minded community and family. We found a deeper appreciation for all of life in the clarity born of our simplicity and growing gratitude for what's truly substantial and important in life. Our family love grew stronger as well as our appreciation for community and cooperative living. Sometimes in order to arrive at a deeper gratitude for what's truly meaningful we have to practice patience and be courageous in the face of the transformative experiences of acute personal change.

PATIENCE

Along with gratitude, patience is one of the greatest powers on earth. Sometimes by not taking action, we take the best action, for events have a wonderful way of working themselves out on their own, if we can remain patient long enough to allow events to unfold naturally.

In our mental and emotional lives we sometimes come under attack by others through force of circumstance, emotional immaturity or misunderstanding. There may be many motives for such aggression directed towards us, but the most common factor is fear. Someone who is cruel, hurtful or aggressive is often fearful underneath.

It's always better to transcend a problem than to directly engage it, for if we raise our own conscious awareness out of the conflict then the aggressor is left alone to face their own aggressive nature. The best we can do, is to understand that our own understanding of others is our greatest protection from their negativity. Understanding is higher than action. And when our understanding is directed by our compassion we can help others find release from the suffering of their own aggression.

Furthermore, no one can actually hurt us without our consent. We allow the hurt of others to touch us when we weaken our understanding of others, allowing their emotional difficulties to enter into our own emotional house. As our emotions become turbulently mixed with another's, we also begin to identify with that emotional turbulence and soon we are allowing ourselves to feel distressed over the situation. You see, we have allowed the negativity to cross the threshold of our own perceptions. If we check the force of negative energies at the door of our own perception we can deny those negativities. We love others best when we impartially understand them and this also protects us from absorbing their negativity.

GANESHA TAUGHT ME PATIENCE

Once when I was on pilgrimage in northern India I visited the ancient city of Vrindhavan. It's a holy site situated on the sacred river Yamuna several hours from Delhi.

There are said to be many thousands of temples there dedicated to Sri Krishna, the playful and beautiful cowherd who spoke the famous Hindu scripture known as the Bhagavad-gita or "*Song of God.*" Indeed the whole town is dedicated to the worship of Sri Krishna and consequently is a very magical, peaceful and spiritually uplifting place.

One day as I was wandering about the markets browsing among the many items I noticed a large array of handmade carvings of the joyful deity Ganesha. In India and throughout the Asian world, Ganesha is the archetypal representation of divine wisdom and luck as well as a remover of obstacles on the path of those seeking self-realization and spiritual knowledge. His images are ubiquitous throughout India and He is loved and admired in all provinces and among all classes and communities.

I've always admired Ganesha's playful image and the auspiciousness He represents, so as I wandered among those images I felt attracted to take an image home with me, but none seemed to touch my heart and inspire a purchase, so I refrained from buying one there, and, dissapointed, went down to the banks of the lovely Yamuna river.

In the afternoons the temperature tends to rise dramatically in India, sometimes up to 120 degrees, so this is an ideal time after lunch to visit the picturesque sandstone ghats along the river's edge and take a respectful and prayerful dip in the cooling waters of the Yamuna, which are said to wash away sin and brighten the soul.

That afternoon as I sat cross-legged in the gentle current I felt at ease with the warm sun at my back and the cool water up to my chest. I recited the Gayatri mantra for about twenty minutes and afterwards as I relaxed there in the water for a few moments, I began to casually dredge the sands before me with my fingertips, raising up the fine sands above the water, examining their glistening quality.

After the third pull my hands struck upon an object that I raised up in delight. It was a 7-inch tall terracotta image of Ganesha seated on a throne. At the moment when I raised it up to the sunlight a great jubilant shout went up amongst my companions and many Indians nearby shouted Jaya! Jaya! When they saw I had found an old image of Ganesha in the river.

It was an exhilarating moment that was both auspicious and delightful. I felt that Ganesha had blessed me, as well as rewarded my patience earlier in the market place. As I mentioned previously my teacher had a saying he often repeated; *"Wait and see.* Often our patience is rewarded in ways that far exceed our initial expectations.

Patience is more than a virtue; it's a very practical consideration as well. Sometimes, with delightful results.

INDUCING GRATITUDE

Think of all the people who have shared abilities, talents, time, and energy with you. Think of the sacrifice of your mother and father, your teachers, mentors and friends.

Deeply appreciate and pray for the well being of all those who gave you powerful experiences, even the ones that were hard to digest, because often these are the experiences we learn the most from.

Look around you and appreciate where you live, and whom you live with. Be grateful for your wife and children. Your brothers and sisters, your husband, your community, the amazing world you live in and the opportunities that are available to you. Cultivate gratitude for this precious human life that affords you the opportunity to seek out deeper realizations.

Be grateful for the immense amounts of information and education that's available via schools and the Internet. Recognize the vast abundance of energy, resources and commodities that surround you on all sides.

Be grateful for all the wonderful varieties of food that are so abundantly available everywhere regardless of season. Be grateful you don't have to go out everyday and hunt, grow or gather your food.

Be grateful for the mobility of your limbs and the incredible range of thoughts, emotions, intelligence and awareness that you use every moment of everyday, every week, every month every year.

Be grateful to be alive!

CHAPTER SEVEN
ABUNDANCE PERSONIFIED

"When everything is done for the center of all beauty,
everything is beautifully done."
-B.R. Sridhar Dev Goswami

All women are beautiful. Not just some who have physically attractive features or a fashionable weight, hair color or attire. The externals change from generation to generation, but within…is the feminine energy or shakti, the feminine creative force that governs the growth and development of all forms.

In previous centuries rubenesque women were considered healthy, wealthy and attractive. Physical abundance was considered an indicator of all other types of abundance and wellbeing. Thin women were considered sickly and weak.

Of course this type of thinking has been reversed in modern times and notably in the mid sixties, it became more fashionable for women to be super thin. Models like Twiggy, ushered in the era of a womanly beauty that was unnaturally thin. Of course, this was a trend that had been waxing and waning throughout the beginning of the 20th century with the decline in popularity of hooped skirts in the late nineteenth century. This misconceived paradigm of fashionably thin continues to be promoted by advertisers. This distorted view of women as objects of pleasure continues its pernicious effect all the more with the addition of digital photographic enhancements and perpetuates an illusion of perfect feminine beauty that few women in real life can live up to. Thankfully, in recent decades men and women are redefining beauty and adopting more natural appearances as well as acceptance of themselves as uniquely beautiful individuals, despite physical flaws and imperfections of nature. Many women no longer shave their legs or use costly cosmetics produced by corporations that are thoughtless towards the environment and abusive to animals.

Despite the media images that we are confronted with most of us realize that it is in the inner conscious identity where true beauty resides. Sadly, some misogynistic cultures and religious fundamentalists still look upon women as the emblem of temptation and sin. But isn't it rather the evil desires within exploitive men that is the true, and greater evil? Like beauty, disdain is also in the eye of the beholder and says more about the person perceiving than that which is perceived.

How could someone who gives us birth, feeds and clothes us, loves us, nourishes us, enhances and enriches our lives in everyway be considered as anything less than sacred? When properly honored by men, women bring out the best in men. Women are the cradle of creation and the personification of devotion, and their dedication, love and selfless action is apparent everywhere, in the couple, the family, the community, and the nation. Woman is the foundation of the world.

Beauty is something inherent in all women for it is the unique potency of the Divine. That which is subtle, beautiful and refined is a closer reflection of the light of Divinity. Women at their best, personify the good qualities of affection, nourishment, kindness, mercy, faith, hope and dedication.

What if, in place of the worn out, bigoted and exploitive male-dominated paradigm of Divinity we arrived at another, more balanced and harmonious conclusion? What if the Divine Reality where to be represented as an infinite play of both masculine and feminine energies, playfully counter-balancing each other in infinite dynamic rounds of bliss producing energetic wheels of unity in diversity?

Perhaps its not enough to merely replace the male-oriented divine paradigm with the feminine, for if we exclusively embrace the feminine without the harmony of the male/female dynamic we will eventually fall into the same abyss of imbalance and gender bias that was produced by the exclusively male-dominated world view and its attendant religious systems. True understanding will follow the example of the natural order where potent male as well as female potency, work together for a greater harmony. Yet science and the deepest understandings of spirituality and psychology demonstrate that the feminine is, in reality, the predominating factor in nature. The Vedic conception honors the feminine characteristics of the non-material self, or spiritual soul, as the atomic anti-material energetic identity at the core of all organic biological manifestations. I would also venture to say that male power should be guided by female wisdom. Not in the worldly sense, but in the subtler, deeper archetypical appreciation of Sophia, Mary, Saraswati, Tara, Lakshmi, Durga and Bhakti Devi. These are the personifications of divine wisdom expressed through gentleness, creativity, service, dedication and ultimately the love of the individual soul for its Divine Source.

This divine feminine figure is to be honored and kept as a high and holy ideal above the degraded consciousness that has led us into a nightmarish world of exploitive destruction. She who is the Mother of all manifestations can never be exploited as the women of the world currently are. She is not an order-carrier for the aggressively ambitious and exploitive male drives that keep us prisoners in a never ending round of unfulfilled lives searching for happiness in the transitory world of the senses. She, The Divine Mother Energy is a super-subjective-spiritually-all-conscious-nourishing-personification of affection, mercy, grace, devotion, creativity and beauty. She is abundance personified, the unlimited matrix, of both matter and consciousness.

What we serve, we place above us, and this tends to uplift us towards that higher ideal. What we exploit and enjoy we place below us, and its exploitation degrades us, whether it be sensory objects, people, the environment or the planet as a whole.

Let us honor all women as the crown of creation. The flowering of felicity, for woman embodies the glorious and nurturing qualities of affection, mercy, grace, devotion, creativity and beauty. As the divine feminine, She is the inspirational light of faith and in this regard She is the open door to absolute abundance of the highest type. She is the absolute abundance of our inherent wisdom nature, our non-material identity in transcendent spiritual consciousness. For our very soul is a feminine potency or Shakti.

As the Great Mother, the Divine Feminine can be conceived in all her varied forms manifest as the unlimited patterns of energy and information found in nature. As such, She is Durga Devi, the regulatrix of all entities and material manifestations. In Her highest personification as devotion and faith, She is Bhakti Devi, the radiance of faith and devotion, which facilitates the transaction of love between the soul and Divinity. She is the affectionate bond between the individual soul and the dynamic Godhead of both feminine and male divine potencies.

Physical appearances are peripheral to our inner necessity, which is our inner hearts search for fulfillment. It is this searching quality within our hearts that is the reflection of our inner substance. Beauty and abundance is an inside job, for all of us, and true wealth is a state of inner fullness, paradoxically found only through our inner necessity or search.

Just as the rising full moon nourishes the plants and herbs causing their sap to rise, similarly the Divine Feminine inspires us with a unique insight and faith that nourishes and transforms the otherwise banal moments of our lives. In such special moments we glimpse the absolute illumination and inner radiance of creation, and are humbled as the miraculous and deeply meaningful nature of life becomes apparent to us. Yet everyday we live in that same miraculous universe, even when on the surface it may not appear so. It is a matter of perspective. We can position ourselves for such moments, but ultimately they are a form of divine grace, a gift of the divine feminine, and a blessing that may come in an unexpected hour. To prepare for such greater insights, the feminine qualities of dedication, selfless devotion, compassion and mercy are indispensable. These qualities are integral to the spiritual path.

In those cherished moments of insight we forget the difficulties, fears and frustrations that harass and distract us. From this higher perspective we can come to realize that enlightenment and other such states of deep insight and joy are not something to be achieved or won through our hard work and iron-jawed willpower, membership in a religious group, ritualistic action, hard austerity or intellectual study.

The achievement of these exalted states of abundant consciousness and insight are in truth a pre-existent state of consciousness within us, an exalted state inherent in our deepest spiritual nature. That wealth is only waiting to be recognized and uncovered. These experiences relate to the essential ground of our being in consciousness. Our inner consciousness is of the nature of that unified field of underlying infinite potentiality, unity in diversity, and ultimate ecstasy. At the deepest level we are success, wisdom and joy, *Sat-Chit-Ananda*. The culture of the divine feminine within us helps us to recover this lost inner wealth.

Such insights of unfolding conscious awareness become apparent when our intensity of inquiry exceeds the depth of their occlusion. Here we may recognize the truth of the statement "Seek and ye shall find." *"Knock, and the door shall be opened to you."* By intensity of purpose we literally penetrate the barrier of our own ignorance and uncover our own hidden treasure of immense potentiality. It is said that sincerity is invincible. As our intensity and sincerity increase, we draw out the mercy, grace and revelation. There's nothing more invincible than a mothers love. .

APPRECIATING MOTHERS EVERYWHERE

It's certainly an understatement to say that mothers of all kinds are central to our growth, nurturing, and well being in this world. Our mother provides us with this physical body to complete our karmas in this life. It is a great gift and one that is delivered to us with great personal sacrifice. Our mothers nurture and love us from the beginning. They sit up with us all night when we are sick, plan our future successes, educate, feed and clothe us. They are always there to cheer us on whether it is our first school play or our command performance. A mother's love is unconditional. As a single mother, my own mother sacrificed so much for me and I am grateful. I will always be grateful to Her.

The purity of a mothers love is unmatched, and the purity and strength of character a mother maintains is transferred to the children, the family, the community, the nation and the world. In that sense we could say that mother is the foundation of this world. If a mother is corrupt, the family quickly deteriorates, good values in society diminish, criminal elements increase and abusive karmas follow, further imploding the society from within.

Motherhood is a sacred responsibility for the physical and emotional nurturing of the children and the family. Her love can also communicate higher values and spiritual ideas to the children ensuring that they will grow up to contribute beauty to the world. If the mother's love is imbued with spiritual wisdom it can assist the family to ultimately transcend material existence through spiritual realization.

THE GREAT MOTHER IN EUROPE

Spring is a time of renewal when the seasons come full circle and is celebrated as a time of rebirth. In Greek mythology, the month of May was first named for Maia, who is also known as "wise one", "grandmother" and "midwife". Her festival was the Festival of Flowers, usually held on May 1st. It is a potent time to remember the Divine Feminine and to acknowledge the interconnection of all things both spiritual and worldly.

This ritual still survives in a hidden way in the Catholic practice of dedicating May 1st to Mother Mary as "Mistress of Spring", "Queen of the Flowers", and "Lady of the Roses." Here we can find clear evidence that Maia embodies the same aspects of the great Mother archetype which were later embodied in the figure of Mary. Just as Maia's son Hermes embodies an earlier manifestation of the archetypal energy later embodied by Mary's son, Jesus.

May first is also an ancient Gaelic festival called Beltaine and is celebrated in Ireland, Scotland and the Isle of Man, though there were similar festivals held at the same time in the other Celtic countries of Wales, Brittany Cornwall and Galicia, where it's known as "Maios" in the local tongue, which is also related to the Greek idea of Maia.

In the Indian Vedic culture, Maia, or Maya is the personified archetypal energy of Mother Nature also known as Durga Devi. All material forms are expressions of the Great Mother's energy, and she is also acknowledged as Vishnu-shakti, the potency of the all-pervading, transcendent sacred source of all Divine Consciousness.

As mentioned previously, Bhakti, or devotional piety is another form of this Divine Mother energy and is the underlying energetic force in all forms of traditional religious expression, yoga, prayer and worship. The Divine Feminine is most often expressed in prayer, devotion and self-giving for the nourishment of others. These are qualities that celebrate life as an expression of spiritual creativity and nourishment for the unity in diversity of all beings in the Universe as a holistic living system.

Maya, or Durga Devi, as the illusory nature of matter, is the material face of the Divine Mother. She nurtures all beings and clothes them in physical forms and is the ground from which all biological forms emerge. She is the shadow of the higher Mother Potency, the feminine Face of Godhead or *Yoga Maya*, the eternal conscious substance from which all forms of consciousness are manifest. The Vedas call Her *ladhini shakti*, the divine-pleasure-potency.

She is reflected in this world in the figure of all women, the holy Tulasi plant, the cow that gives us milk, the guru and guide, Mother Ganges, the most sacred river of Indian culture that liberates all souls and *Bhakti Devi*, the personification of faith, and the devotional potency that leads our hearts to unfold in devotional love of Divinity. She is actually inconceivable and unlimited, an inexhaustible subjective Reality of infinite potentiality, also personified as Lakshmi Devi the Goddess of Fortune.

Sri Lakshmi Devi is unlimited auspiciousness, abundance and beauty. As the personified creative function she appears as Saraswati Devi, in this form She is also personified wisdom, beauty and sacred sound. In the ancient histories of India she appears in unlimited forms such as Yasoda, Saci, Draupadi Parvati, and Vishnupriya. In Christianity she is personified in the person of Mary.

Wherever we find Mercy, Grace, Compassion, Beauty, Nurturing, Kindness, Faith and Love...Mother will be there in some form. Mother is unlimited. Mother is compassionate. Mother is Mercy.

Honor your Mother. She is a sacred Deity. There's nothing more abundant than a sincere Mothers love.

TULASI AS THE NATURAL DIVINE

The current environmental disasters we are witnessing around the world are evidence of mankind's disregard for his sacred relation with the natural environment. This ignorance takes the form of gross exploitation and results in widespread environmental damage compromising the quality of life for all living beings upon the Earth. Fortunately, all over the world people are beginning to return to a paradigm of reverence towards the environment. A natural lifestyle is one that honors all life and safeguards the purity of the environment as a spiritual culture. This is a sustainable and healthy lifestyle. This is deep ecology that honors and protects the environment by nurturing enlightened qualities in the individual.

In the Indian spiritual traditions the tulasi plant is regarded as a symbol of divinity and holds a preeminent place as the ultimate symbol of purity and human relations with the Divine Source. Tulasi is a Sanskrit word which literally means, *"the one that has no equals."* It is the one, which has no comparison, matchless, and the one whose merits are invaluable. Tulasi is considered a very sacred and divine plant that has both physical and spiritual healing properties. Since time immemorial, tulasi has been worshipped as a Deity, and an expression of the Great Goddess in Indian spiritual culture. In ancient times, and even to this day, the presence of tulasi in a house was considered as a symbol of spiritual merit of that family.

Tulasi is a *sattvic* plant and it is said that by honoring the tulasi plant and wearing tulasi beads, a person will improve their sattvic nature of goodness. In India and wherever Hindu culture is present we find people wearing *tulasi mala*, a necklace made out of tulasi beads around their neck, especially while performing mantra meditation and also during divine worship to ward off negative thoughts and evil influences.

The tulasi plant, with its leaves of unique and strong fragrance, is said to cleanse the environment and provide a healthy and peaceful atmosphere. It is said that the tulasi plant releases copious oxygen into the atmosphere and it is considered to be beneficial to sleep in the sacred and healthy ambience of the holy tulasi plant. It is also believed that the presence of tulasi will ward off negative subtle entities from entering the house. During an eclipse we find people placing tulasi leaves in stored water and food to prevent them from getting contaminated due to the inauspiciousness caused by the eclipse. In view of its potential properties to cleanse the atmosphere, in India, tulasi is liberally grown in industrial areas for prevention of pollution. Agriculture that is fumigated with the dried tulasi plant repels insects.

The tulasi plant in its entirety is extensively used in Ayurveda in curing various diseases like allergy, skin infections, cold, cough and respiratory infections, heart diseases, stomach disorders, sore throat, ear ache, mouth infections, fever, headache and sleeplessness.

It is said to be very effective in viral infections and malaria as well. In Ayurveda tulasi is also considered very effective for use as an anti-bacterial, antiseptic, anti-fungal, anti-viral, and anti-allergic, and is considered as an immune-stimulant. Considered as the queen of all herbs, the Vedas declare that where tulasi is, there is welfare, health and abundance.

The glory of tulasi is mentioned in several puranas, which are the ancient histories of Vedic culture. The *Padma Purana, Brahma Vaivartha Purana, Skandha Purana, Garuda Purana, Kartheeka Purana and Vishnu Purana,* all extol the great virtues of tulasi. In the *Padma Purana* it is said that tulasi came out from the joyous tears of Maha-Vishnu that fell on the divine nectar or amrita that emerged from the churning of the great ocean by the devas and asuras.

According to ayurveda, the entire tulasi plant, leaves, flowers, stems, roots, seeds and even the soil surrounding the tulasi roots, are all full of spiritual and medicinal significance.

Abundance flows where tulasi grows, for she represents Lakshmi Devi, the Goddess of Fortune, and is considered *sri lakshmi swarupam* symbolizing the very form of Lakshmi Devi. It is said that where tulasi is, there also will all-pervading Vishnu reside and as such, that place is considered as a holy *tirtha*, a sacred place where the spiritual world intersects with the material.

In ancient times and even to day in traditional Hindu families throughout the world we find women praying and walking round the tulasi plant, pouring water daily in the morning and evening for the welfare of her husband and family.

No Hindu house would be without a tulasi plant in their courtyard. Tulasi, the perennial symbol of Hindu philosophy, tradition, culture and heritage is Nature's gift to mankind. The Vedas refer to tulasi as a *kalpa vriksha* or a heavenly wish fulfilling tree on earth.

LAKSHMI DEVI - GODDESS OF ABUNDANCE

Lakshmi Devi is the Hindu Goddess of Fortune who is said to govern all forms of wealth, success and prosperity. She is also known as Lady Luck, and in fact our word "lucky" comes from Her name Lakshmi, which is pronounced as "luckie in the Hindi language. In India she is casually called Lucky Devi. As the potency or *shakti* and consort of Lord Vishnu, the divine expression of universal preservation, Lakshmi Devi is also the goddess of health and beauty. Sri Lakshmi embodies sublime beauty, perfections, peace, strength, victory, auspiciousness, opulence and wisdom. Because Lakshmi possesses all of these good and noble qualities, She embodies infinite wealth, indicating that good and noble qualities are the only wealth we can truly keep. Lakshmi Devi is always depicted sitting or standing on a lotus with golden coins flowing in an endless stream from one of her hands, symbolic of when the lotus of wisdom blossoms, the wealth of good and noble qualities appears and Lakshmi's blessings are present.

Lakshmi is also called Shri, which means *"the beautiful"*, and Her images are found in Jain and Buddhist monuments, as well as Hindu temples. She is analogous to the Greek Aphrodite and Roman Venus - who in mythology also originated from the oceans - she is generally thought of as the personification of material fortune, beauty and prosperity.

Whenever Vishnu appears in this world in one of His many incarnations for the teaching of Dharma, deliverance of the pious and the destruction of evil, Lakshmi also appears with Him.

According to the Vishnu Purana, Lakshmi is the power and potency of Lord Vishnu. This is consonant with the basic philosophy of Sri Vaishnavism which honours Sri Lakshmi as the *iswarim sarva bhootanam*, or the supreme goddess not merely the goddess of wealth.

VAIKUNTHA- FREEDOM FROM ANXIETY

When the individual soul realizes to a greater extent the inherent abundance of its own spiritual existence, she undergoes a transformation from the karmic experiences of action and reaction to the clear insight of awakened consciousness, This state is conspicuous by its freedom from afflicted emotions and congnitive obscurations. It is often expressed as dedicated service and self-giving. This conscious transition from exploitation to dedication marks the entrance of the individual into the plane of consciousness known in yogic literature as Vaikuntha, or the plane beyond all anxiety and suffering. Various Sanskrit terms can express similar states that are free from suffering such as nirvana and moksha. Yet, the term Vaikuntha denotes not merely the cessation of suffering but the positive engagement of loving service as well. It is a plane of self-dedication wherein the consciousness unfolds into deeper levels of divine abundance.

In the symbolic mythology of India, Vaikuntha is the divine realm beyond material manifestation where unlimited numbers of joyful liberated souls enjoy the abundantly opulent loving service of the divine couple, Lakshmi-Narayana, who are the spiritual personifications of divine Godhead in full expression of infinite wealth, beauty, strength, detachment, wisdom, mystic potencies and brilliant glory. The word Vaikuntha means *"without anxiety"*. The Vedas explain it not as a geographic location, but a plane of soul consciousness where there is an infinite expanse of transcendental sky filled with unlimited spiritual planets populated by unlimited perfected souls celebrating ecstatic eternal spiritual existence in joyful loving service to the divine couple in unlimited transcendental forms of variety and expression. In Vaikuntha there are unlimited spiritual forms, cities, communities and full variegated manifestations there, yet they are all composed of *sat-chit-ananda,* which means conscious existence, full awareness and ever increasing spiritual joy.

The whole atmosphere is predominated by radiant goodness and a supportive nurturing happiness. There is no passing of time, for all is existing in the eternal present. All is self-illuminated by clear consciousness, and as such there is no decay or anything of an unclean or unwholesome nature. All is brilliant, self-illuminated transcendent conscious glory. All actions here in samsara, or material existence, produce reactions that ultimately lead to division and decay. This is the realm of karma, or action and reaction. There, all actions produce ever-increasing joy and greater unity and love. We can bring this Vaikuntha consciousness into manifestation on this outer plane of matter by raising our own consciousness, individually, communally, nationally and globally. A greater ideal as the paradigm of what is possible is the primitive bud of such expression in the world. Physicists have demonstrated the actual empty nature of all phenomena revealing that matter and phenomena are really nothing more than patterns of energy that are inherently linked in codependence with the consciousness that perceives them.

Eutopian? Yes. And why not? Should we not aspire to a greater life of harmony for all living beings? We have the power to rethink and reinvent our world. It can be so if we aspire for it. Thinking makes it so. As a race if every man woman and child were to retrain their minds in a positive way we could change the world for better overnight.

DIWALI - THE FESTIVAL OF LIGHTS

In India, there is a festival of lights called Diwali. It is an expression of this vaikuntha ideal dating back thousands of years in Indian culture. The festival is celebrated throughout the country with fervor and joy to dispel the darkness and herald the light of spiritual understanding. The name Diwali is based on the Sanskrit word "Deepavali" – "*Deepa*" meaning light and "*Avali*" meaning a row, signifies a row of lights. Every home is lit with the orange glow of twinkling lamps to welcome Lakshmi, the goddess of wealth and prosperity. Diwali is an annual festival, which leads us into the Truth and Light. It is celebrated across the length and breadth of India and symbolizes the vanquishing of ignorance, and the light of wisdom that drives away darkness. Diwali is celebrated on the 15th day of the dark fortnight of the months of October and November every year throughout the world by over a billion Hindus.

As the "festival of lights" it is a common practice at Diwali to light small oil lamps and place them around homes, courtyards, verandahs and gardens as well as on rooftops and outer walls. The exchange of sweets and the explosion of fireworks also accompany the celebration of this lavish and colorful festival. Houses and business premises are also renovated and decorated, and entrances are made colorful with lovely traditional motifs of rangoli designs to welcome Lakshmi, the Goddess of wealth and prosperity. All entryways are decorated for her welcome, as the consort of Lord Vishnu, who is the all-pervading representation of divine preservation. Lakshmi Devi is also the goddess of health and beauty. Sri Lakshmi embodies sublime beauty, perfections, peace, strength, balance, auspiciousness, opulence and wisdom.

As a female counterpart of the preserving aspect of Divinity, Mother Lakshmi is also called "Shri", the female potency of the Supreme Being. Goddess Lakshmi means "Good Luck" to Hindus. The word "Lakshmi" is derived from the Sanskrit word "Laksya", meaning 'aim' or 'goal', and she is the goddess of all types of abundance, both material and spiritual. Also lakh, which means "one hundred thousand' as a monetary unit in India, is the first part of Lakshmi's name, symbolizing her blessings that pour forth abundantly. To indicate her long-awaited arrival, small footprints are drawn with rice flour and vermilion powder all over the house, and lamps are kept burning all through the night. Lakshmi-puja is performed in the evening when tiny lamps of clay are lighted to drive away inauspiciousness. Bhajans in praise of Ma Lakshmi are sung and food preparations and traditional sweets are offered to the Goddess.

On the day of Diwali the sun enters its second course and passes Libra, which is represented by the balance or scale. Hence, this design of Libra is believed to have suggested the balancing of account books and their closing on this day. Despite the fact this day falls on the dark moon day it is regarded as the most auspicious. Everywhere in India the strains of joyous sounds of bells and drums float from the temples as people everywhere are invoking the Goddess Lakshmi Devi with devotional songs and offerings of sweets.

Hindus believe a divine light of knowledge dawns upon humanity at Diwali time as the devotional mood conquers material ignorance. This self-enlightenment is metaphorically expressed through the flickering lamps illuminating the humble homes of the poor as well as the stately abodes of the wealthy. On this day Lakshmi is said to walk through the fields and stroll the streets, showering her blessings on all people for plenty and prosperity. When the sun sets in the evening and the ceremonial worship is complete, all the offerings of homemade sweets are distributed as *prashadam,* meaning *"Her Mercy."* Family and community feasts are arranged and gifts are exchanged. Also, well-dressed men, women and children go to temples and fairs, and visit friends and relatives.

The Diwali festival is a beautiful celebration of abundance and the interconnection of all life through the medium of gratitude. It demonstrates our dependence upon the divine energetic relation of all things. It's also a beautiful paradigm of abundant sharing, appreciation and gratitude. It transforms the paradigm of exploitation into a living expression of devotional gratitude that invites ever more abundant energy to flow through our lives, nourishing us spiritually on the inside and materially on the outside.

When we honor all things as expressions of divine consciousness, we impart a higher dynamic value to everything that enriches our lives as we handle these energies. Every forest becomes holy, every mountain sacred, every heart becomes a sacred temple of the Divine, and every coin is a symbol of divine and unlimited abundance. All abundance ultimately is meant for divine service and the glory of the Whole, the One, the Spiritual Family of Life, of which we are all a part of. When we exploit energies we place them below us. We devalue them spiritually to mere material commodities to be moved from point A to point B, or selfishly absorbed for our own gratification. I choose to acknowledge that the purpose of human life is to grow and contribute to the whole. Sincerely work with what you've got, and when more arrives be grateful and reinvest it in the service of others. Currency of any kind is an energetic flow from one state to another. Gratitude and service are what keeps the energy in a circular motion. If you're stuck, start giving, and watch the flow return.

FULFILLMENT IN LOVE

Aligning our hearts in spiritual love is a natural adjustment and has been delineated in the ancient yogic traditions as the ultimate aim of human life. The Upanishads define the self as an eternal, non-material, consciousness, distinct from biological manifestations. The soul is observed as an eternal unit of conscious awareness that according to it's desires, takes birth by entering material forms. The soul remains essentially unchanged as the body grows, transforms, dwindles and passes away through linear time. The conscious self continues to exist independent of material manifestation and destruction, and carries with it its desires and aspirations from one life to the next. It is of the nature of eternal existence, awareness and ecstasy. The food of the soul is said to be spiritual loving exchanges *(rasa)*.

Despite the eternal soul's involvement with matter, it can liberate itself from the cycles of birth and death by internally altering its desires from a material to spiritual orientation. Through service, devotion and a spiritually elevated clearing of consciousness, the soul can rise above matter and regain its eternal status and revive its forgotten relationship of spiritual love with its Divine

Source. This is the essence of spiritual wisdom, regardless of which culture one may be born into or outward religious affiliation one may be affiliated with. We are all seeking fulfillment, happiness and pleasure through the objects of the senses. Yet whatever we acquire here has a beginning and an end. There is no duration or lasting satisfaction and happiness in the objects of the senses or material acquisitions. For whatever we gain in life will all be lost at the time of death. Everything here is changing from one state to another and is ruled by the great law of impermanence. When we cling to what is by nature impermanent we are destined to suffer. Perhaps a deeper more refined acquisition needs to be sought, that of spiritual attainment, self-realization and the understanding that ultimately our lasting fulfillment can never be found in what is temporarily manifest through matter. True wealth is inner contentment within the non-material, unchanging transcendent self. To know oneself in this way, in truth is to realize one's greater potentiality. The subjective evolution of consciousness provides a systematic, scientific and measurable approach to the practical problems of life and the realization of their solution in spiritual consciousness.

Spiritual love affords us a higher liberty of conscious awareness and freedom in realization of our deeper consciousness. It is our very nature to love and the addition or subtraction of everything in this world can never change or alter this truth, though it may cover or occlude it temporarily. We are children of that eternal ground of substantial conscious reality. Our fulfillment and happiness are realized in our return to that conscious reality, and we will ultimately never be satisfied with anything but that reality. We are meant to love, and our love is perfected when it is realized in our eternal relationship with each other in service to the reality of the whole. Our true fulfillment is in love alone. By practicing generosity we insure that the cyclical flow of energies will continue to come towards us, as well as flow away from us to benefit others. Gratitude is the greatest way to pray, for it honors what we have been given and transforms our very nature into a state of abundance personified. Gratitude is the antidote for neediness and poverty. Realizing unconditional love by culturing loving kindness, compassion, balance and empathetic joy for the happiness of others frees our hearts and minds from malice and self-imposed sufferings.

My teacher, Srila Sridhar Maharaja once said:

> *"Movement means to give love... that is the conception of service. No one is taking any love, but they're all capitalists, investing in love. Everyone's a capitalist in his own position. He is contributing and they don't want to take it back. So opulence is there. Where all the members are contributing then there will be opulence. So in the land of opulence there's no want... all are givers. Stealthily one is giving but not taking stealthily. This is Vaikuntha consciousness, a plane of dedication where all are givers. All have compassion and kindness for each other."*

Everyday try to contribute something of value for the benefit and well-being of others. By doing so you can also direct your service to the Divine presence in the heart of all beings. By giving in this way you be assured that you have fulfilled the purpose of human life. By contributing to the well-being of others, we serve the well-being of the Earth. By seeking the Divine in each other, we discover the Divine within ourselves. If you can skillfully do this in a way that does not draw attention to yourself and in a way that honors all, it's even better. It makes no difference if you are rich or famous, high or low, wise or foolish, beautiful or plain.

It's the sincerity in our hearts that counts in the end, not the external incidentals. And that sincerity is best expressed through unconditional love, love for all living beings and love that honors the Sacred Source of all life and manifestation. This is the essence of Absolute Abundance. This is a path with heart.

Absolute Abundance

ABOUT THE AUTHOR

In the spring of 1985, as a young man in search of answers, Matthew Bennett traveled alone to India and met his Gurudeva, the venerable sanskrit scholar, vaisnava saint, and eminent Vedic Acharya- Srila Sridhar Maharaja (1895-1988). The following year, on the banks of the holy Ganges river, Matthew was initiated into the brahminical lineage of priest-teachers, and given the name Matura Nath das. Inspired by the deep wisdom and devotion of his Gurudeva, Matura has engaged in educational outreach programs for the past 28 years. He has taught over 1200 classes and led numerous kirtans in India, England, Australia and America.

As an Ayurvedic Counselor certified by The American Institute of Vedic Studies under Dr. David Frawley, Matura assists others to find clarity and growth through the insight born of self-awareness, Ayurveda and Vedic Devotional Yoga. Matura has dedicated his life to helping others heal body, mind and spirit in order to assist in the achievement of greater levels of satisfaction and success in all areas of life.

For more information or to schedule a private consultation.

Please visit
www.abundantlives.org

Matura Matthew Bennett is also a multi-instrumentalist who plays sitar, harmonium, flute, and guitar. He sings a wide variety of original songs and sanskrit chants that heal, inspire and delight the soul. Songs from his new cd "Dharma Wheels" as well as his first cd "Artistic-2-Mystic can be found online at amazon, itunes, cd baby and other outlets.

His music website is: www.reverbnation.com/matura

10462704R00135

Made in the USA
San Bernardino, CA
16 April 2014